OILS

JOSE M. PARRAMON

Parramón editions

Published by Parramón Ediciones, S.A.
Lepanto, 264 - 4.º - Barcelona - (Spain)

© José M.ª Parramón Vilasaló
Second impression

Register Book Number: 785
Legal Deposit: B. 13.056-84
ISBN: 0 86343 030 9

Printed in Spain by
GENERAL GRAFIC, S.A.
Caspe, 172 - Barcelona-13 - Spain

Distributed in the United Kingdom by
FOUNTAIN PRESS LTD.
65, Victoria Street,
Windsor, Berkshire SL41 EH

All correspondece concerting the content of this volume should
be adressed to Parramón Ediciones, S.A.

'Painting and Drawing' Series

Distributors in U. K.

FOUNTAIN PRESS LTD

65, Victoria Street, Windsor, Berkshire SL4 1EH
Telephone: Windsor 56959

CONTENT

STUDY OF MATERIALS

It happened in Bruges, the capital of Western Flanders in Northern Belgium.

The year was 1420.

One day the painter Jan van Eyck, who at that time, was better known as «Jan of Bruges», was talking to a group of contemporary artists in his studio.

He was talking in Flemish:

«We are still painting just as they did a hundred, two hundred, even three hundred years ago with all the Gothic prejudices and traditional rules: placing the figures on glittering, empty backgrounds, lifeless and contrary to reality and truth. So I suggest that we paint men, women, trees and fields as they really are. I suggest that we paint scenes from ordinary life, the true life around us.»

The group agreed. It included the Maestro de Flemalle, the celebrated Van der Weyden and the young Petrus Christus. All were talking Flemish and from then on they all tried to paint with the realism recommended by Jan of Bruges.

They formed a school, the famous *Flemish School* which was carried on and strengthened over the years by Bouts, van Goes, Memlink, Bosch... Breugel, Rubens, van Dyck, Jordaens, Rembrandt...

«The Virgin with Child and Angels» (1272) by the Florentine artist Cimbau-be (The Louvre, Paris). Cimbaube is considered to be one of the artists who made great efforts to humanise Gothic art by giving it more expression. Nevertheless, his style reflects the classic features of Gothic painting: figures on a golden, unrealistic background, with stylised expressions and positions, forming a conventional composition. The features remained unchanged until 1300 when Giotto, the great modern Gothic artist, appeared on the scene.

It is not surprising that Jan of Bruges became the founder of a movement which, in the form of the Flemish School, had so much impact upon the artistic world. He had already proved to have an exceptional mind when ten years before, in 1410, he made a discovery which was to change the whole course of the History of Art.

Until 1410 every artist painted his boards and altarpieces with egg tempera. Many years before it had been found that if a coat of oil was applied over the egg tempera, the colours revived and recovered the strength and brilliance of newly painted works. The book «Diversarum artium schedula», written as early as 1200 by the monk Teofilo, had recommended that a coat of olive-oil should be applied over the tempera. However, it was very difficult to dry olive-oil and the painting had to be placed in the sun for several hours and even days, which involved a risk that the painting would deteriorate, the colours darken and the whites lose their strength.

According to the legend, one day Jan van Eyck placed a painting in

«Portrait of Arnolfini and his wife» painted by Jan van Eyck in 1434 (National Gallery, London). One of the most famous paintings by this great Flemish artist which represents a new style coinciding with the beginning of the Renaissance. In this work the artist applies the principles of the Flemish School which he founded and popularised. It shows the full splendour of the «reality» recommended by van Eyck. The careful study of each background detail proves how concerned the artist was to reproduce the pure reality of the objects and furnishings which form part of men's lives. The cold accuracy of the forms appears to be veiled in vibrant light, creating a genuine ambient atmosphere.

---

the sun to dry as Teofilo recommended and when he came to take it in after some hours, he was furious to find that the picture had split.

From then on Jan van Eyck never ceased to search for an oil which would dry in the shade. First he found that linseed oil and nut-oil dried comparatively easily but it was some time before he discovered that if a small amount of «Bruges white varnish» is mixed with linseed oil, this produces a solution which dries easily in the shade, forming a varnish. (We now know that the «Bruges white varnish» was a kind of turpentine similar to that used nowadays for thinning oil colours.)

Van Eyck then tried to dissolve in linseed oil and Bruges white varnish the raw colours used for tempera painting. He found that the colours could be applied in transparent washes or opaque coats which, while drying, could correct shades and colours without destroying their original strength and brilliance and also that they dried perfectly without the painting having to be placed in the sun.

This was the great step forward: Jan van Eyck, the founder of the Flemish School, had discovered the best painting medium, the «royal» medium — oil painting.

GENERAL FEATURES OF OIL-PAINTING

COMPOSITION OF OIL COLOURS

Generally speaking, we can say that nowadays when we artists paint in oils, we use essentially the same ingredients as those employed by Jan van Eyck five hundred years ago, that is:

> *a) COLOURS OR PIGMENTS, which are solid and usually in powder form; they are divided into two categories, the organic, obtained from vegetables and animals, and inorganic, obtained from minerals.*
>
> *b) ADHESIVES or liquid substances which are produced from fatty oils and chemicals, as well as resins, balsams and wax.*

The colours or pigments referred to here are not exclusive to oil-painting, that is to say that they are common to all techniques employed to produce any type of colours, watercolour, tempera, wax, pastilles or oils. They are powdered colours which when mixed and cemented with water, gum arabic, honey and glycerine, for example, provide watercolours; when cemented with water, gum substances and oils, they provide pastel colours and, more to our purpose here, when ground and cemented with fatty oils and chemicals, resins, balsams and waxes, they give us oil-paints.

We should remember, in fact, that Van Eyck did not discover the actual pigments but the cementing substance, the oils which, since his discovery, have enabled artists to «paint in oils».

THE COLOURS

By colours we mean the powdered pigments.

These can be divided into the whites, yellows, reds, blues, greens, browns and blacks.

1. WHITES

The most commonly known are white lead (or silver white), zinc white and titanium white.

WHITE LEAD OR SILVER WHITE. This has an astonishing degree of opacity and strength as a covering substance as well as being very quick-drying. These qualities can be very useful when employing the technique of thick, paste-like coats; it is also suitable for backgrounds or first coats. It is highly poisonous and this should always be remembered, especially when the artist is trying to grind his own colours, since serious consequences can result merely by inhaling the powder. It is not used for watercolours.

ZINC WHITE. This has a colder tone than white lead, is less compact and opaque and also takes longer to dry. This latter feature can be an advantage when an artist is painting a picture which requires several sessions, and prefers to work on an undercoat which is not completely dry. It is not poisonous.

TITANIUM WHITE. In comparison with the other two, this is a modern pigment with a strong colouring power. It possesses normal opacity and dries in average time without any real drawbacks. It is thus very popular with most artists.

In oil-painting, as in any other opaque technique (tempera or pastels), white is one of the most frequently used colours and so the tubes of white oils are generally larger than those of other colours.

2. YELLOWS

The most common can be said to be: Naples yellow, chrome yellow, cadmium yellow, yellow ochre and raw sienna.

NAPLES YELLOW. This is obtained from lead antimonate and is one of the oldest colours: it is opaque and dries quickly. Like all lead pigments, it is poisonous. It can be mixed with any other colour without trouble provided that it is pure and of good quality. Rubens preferred to use it, especially for flesh-tints.

CHROME YELLOW. Obtained from lead and thus poisonous. There are several shades ranging from a very bright lemonish colour to a very dark, almost orange shade. It is opaque and dries quickly but is easily affected by light, tending to darken over the years, especially the lighter shades.

CADMIUM YELLOW. A good strong, brilliant colour, which dries rather slowly. It can be mixed with every colour except the copper pigments.

It is unsuitable for open-air painting but it is excellent and very popular for oil-painting.

YELLOW OCHRE. An earth pigment and one of the oldest. It has great colouring and covering power and can safely and easily be mixed with any other colour provided that it is pure. It is also produced artificially without losing any of these qualities.

RAW SIENNA. Another earth pigment, made from soil from Siena (Italy). It is a beautiful and brilliant colour which, in its oil form, is liable to darken, since it has to be diluted with a lot of oil. So, when painting in oils, it is not advisable to use natural sienna for extensive undersurfaces or for large areas in which it is employed as an ingredient. However, it is an excellent pigment when the cementing substance does not need oil, for instance as tempera.

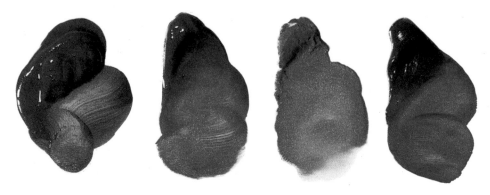

3. REDS

Among the most commonly used, we can mention: burnt sienna, vermilion, cadmium red and madder lake.

BURNT SIENNA. This has the same characteristics as raw sienna but is darker with a reddish tinge. It can be used in every technique, including oil-painting, without the drawbacks of raw sienna, i.e. with less danger of subsequent darkening. It was widely used by the old masters, primarily the Venetians. Some writers claim that it was the colour employed by Rubens for painting the brilliant reds and reflected highlights of his flesh-tints.

VERMILION. A luminous red pigment obtained from minerals and also produced artificially. It covers well but does not dry easily. It is used in every technique but has the sole drawback that it is liable to darken if exposed to the sun. It is inadvisable to mix it with copper pigments and white lead.

CADMIUM RED. This is preferable to vermilion since it does not darken when exposed to the sun. A brilliant, powerful colour, it can be mixed with any other colour, except copper pigments such as opaque green.

MADDER LAKE. An extremely powerful colour, providing a rich range of reddish, purple and carmine tones. It is very liquid, dries slowly and is suitable for every technique except frescoes.

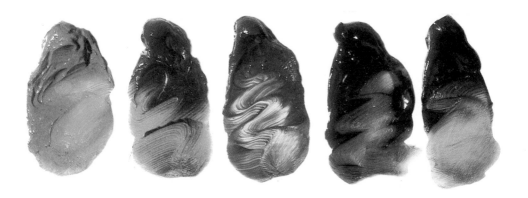

4. BLUES AND GREENS

The most popular are: terra verde, permanent green, viridian green, cobalt blue, ultramarine blue and Prussian blue.

TERRA VERDE. Obtained from ochre, this produces a brownish, khaki green. A very old colour which can be used for every technique: dries comparatively quickly and has good covering power.

PERMANENT GREEN. A bright luminous green produced from a mixture of oxide of chrome (viridian or emeraude green) and cadmium lemon yellow. A safe pigment without any drawbacks.

VIRIDIAN. Also known as emeraude green, this should not be confused with emerald green (Veronese green) which has many drawbacks. Viridian, or emeraude green, is considered the best of the greens due to its tonal range and richness, its permanency and safety.

COBALT BLUE. This is a metallic non-poisonous pigment which can safely be used for every technique. It covers well and dries quickly, which can be inconvenient when it is applied over coats which are not very dry, producing cracks. As an oil-colour it can in time acquire a slight greenish tint due to the amount of oil it requires. Both a light and dark shade are available.

ULTRAMARINE BLUE. Like cobalt, this blue has been used since ancient times. It is obtained from lapis lazuli, a semi-precious stone, and thus was formerly the most expensive colour but it is now produced artificially. It is completely permanent, has average opacity and requires normal drying time: suitable for every technique except frescoes in the open where the colour decomposes. It is available in dark and light shades and in some cases has a more reddish tinge than cobalt blue.

PRUSSIAN BLUE. Also called Paris blue, this transparent pigment has a strong colouring power and dries well. Its greatest drawback is that it is affected by light, which can destroy its colour (but the colour

is regained when placed in darkness for some time). It is inadvisable to mix it with vermilion or zinc white.

5. BROWNS

The most widely used are: raw and burnt umber, Vandyke brown.

RAW AND BURNT UMBER. Both pigments are natural earths and a by-product of calcination. They are both very dark, but the raw umber has a slight greenish tint while the burnt shade is slightly reddish. They can be used for every technique, but darkening is unavoidable over a period. They dry very quickly and so it is inadvisable to apply them in thick coats in order to prevent cracking.

VANDYKE BROWN. A dark tone similar to the umbers but with a rather greyish tinge. It cannot be recommended for painting undercoats in oils since it cracks easily. It can be used for final coats, retouching and in mixtures for rather smaller areas, but is safer in watercolours than in oils. It becomes a cold dirty grey in the open air.

6. BLACKS

The best-known are lamp black and ivory black.

LAMP BLACK. A rather cold shade, it is permanent and can be used for every technique.

IVORY BLACK. A slightly warm shade, it may perhaps provide a deeper black than the above and is also suitable for every type of painting.

THE OILS

LINSEED OIL. This is a fatty oil. It is obtained from flax seeds and produced by «cold drawing» them, that is to say by pressing them without heat, which provides the most suitable oil for painting. It has

CHART OF THE MOST COMMONLY USED OIL-COLOURS

Lemon Cadmium yellow	Medium Cadmium yellow	Yellow ochre
Natural sienna	Burnt sienna	Dark burnt earth
Medium Cadmium red	* Dark madder lake	* Emerald green
* Dark cobalt blue	* Dark ultramarine	Titian blue

Titanium white must be added to this list

a bright yellow colour and dries well (in three or four days) but it must be pure and clean to prevent the colours from darkening. It is used for dissolving and cementing the colours and the amounts added vary according to the structure and fineness of the pigments. It is also employed as a solvent during the actual painting, and in some formulae for printing, i.e. in preparing fabrics, papers, boards, etc. for oil painting.

The fatty oils used in oil-painting also include nut-oil and poppy oil, both of which dry more slowly.

ESSENCE OF TURPENTINE. This is a floating vegetable oil, commonly known as white spirit. It is white and clear and gives off a strong pleasant aromatic smell. When in contact with air, it dries rapidly by evaporation. Essence of turpentine is not a cementing substance in the strict sense of the word but an unbeatable liquid for diluting pigments and dissolving balsams, resins and waxes. It is also the best thinning substance for oil-colours while painting: we shall discuss this later.

MASTIC AND DAMMAR-RESIN. These resins are used in oil-painting as varnishes and diluents to prevent wrinkles, films and subsequent contraction and damage when the painting dries «from within». When heated in a double boiler, it blends with essence of turpentine.

BEESWAX. This pure wax is used in oil-painting as a cementing substance for tube colours, preventing the oil and the pigments from separating, and thus removing the risk of the colours drying or solidifying in the tube. It also causes better colour consistency. 2% of wax heated and blended with essence of turpentine is enough.

I think this description of pigments and oils is sufficient to give you enough idea of the characteristics and composition of oil-paints. I could go on and give some formulae of the substances used as cements and then explain how colours are ground, what sort of utensils are needed, what proportion of oil must be added to each colour, and so on until you could begin to produce your own colours. But do you really need to know all that?

THE SOLUTION TO AN OLD DILEMMA

Is it advisable for an amateur or professional artist to learn how to make his own colours? Nowadays, does he really need to know this?

If you consult any book on painting techniques and materials, you will be forced to conclude that, following the example of the old masters, you should certainly make your own paints, spurning the idea of buying them ready-made since these cannot guarantee absolutely pure quality; it is also claimed that within a few years your paintings will become yellow and stale, the colours will darken, the picture will crack, and so on.

However, if you want to find practical support for this idea by visiting studios and asking expert and famous painters, you will discover that none of these modern artists make their own oil-paints. Without exception, they buy them ready-made from the specialist shops. This is so significant and so much at variance with the books, that it is worth explaining more clearly.

When referring to the studios or workshops of the old masters, from Van Eyck to Goya by way of Titian, Leonardo da Vinci, Michelangelo, Raphael, Velasquez, El Greco, Rubens and Rembrandt, every ancient document and book describes their studio as a large building which either contains or adjoins a kind of kitchen or rudimentary laboratory in which the artist produced his oil-paints and tempera colours, prepared solutions for frescoes, etc.

With Maurice Bossuet, who is very knowledgeable on this subject, we can visualise in these «kitchens», a number of shelves with labelled bottles and vials, each containing one powdered colour or pigment. On well-protected and firmly sealed bottles in a rather dark corner, we would have been able to read names which are still found nowadays on the colour charts of modern manufacturers: «White lead, Naples yellow, Viridian, Ultramarine blue», etc. and near them, in earthenware jars, a number of liquids and products, oils and varnishes with such familiar names as «linseed oil, nut-oil, mastic, turpentine, virgin wax», etc.

In one corner there would be a furnace going and in the middle, in front of the shelves, a strong table with a porphyry top. Beside it

An artist grinding pigments in the 17th Century, after Ryckaert. (An engraving by Maurice Bousset.)

would be placed various mortars, grinders, spatulas, brushes, graduated tubes, etc.

The actual manufacturing process is not particularly difficult: it is a question of diluting the powdered pigments or lumps with oil, by grinding them by hand in the mortar or on the table with a pestle after having prepared the oil by adding varnish and wax: this is pure manual labour which must undoubtedly have taken the artist some hours.

In every case the difficulty is to obtain first-class results and to test one or more formulae which are suitable for the artist's style and which also provide some degree of certainty with regard to drying times, lack of variation, permanency, firmness, etc. Judging by the number of formulae which have been reprinted in books, it is not too much to say that every artist had his own favourite system: thus while Leonardo «carried out many tests, using different oils», Dürer «used nut-oil which he filtered through sifted charcoal». Titian «employed essence of lavender and poppy oil, bleached in the sun» but Rubens «painted with copal varnish, poppy oil and essence of lavender». (Quoted from Max Doerner and Maurice Bousset).

This purely mechanical experimenting which in some cases was certainly successful, but in others completely ineffective, continued until the middle of the last century, when, in this field too, the industrial revolution brought its changes: the first small factories were established for manufacturing paints. It is not surprising that either through inexperience or lack of scruples, some of these early concerns produced unsatisfactory and even extremely bad colours which within a few years turned yellow or black, or could not be mixed with others, etc. Unfortunately, these early stages coincided with one of the most spectacular movements of modern painting, namely impressionism, which sometimes required heavy impastoes, thick coats, flat undersurfaces and brilliant, luminous colours. The inevitable occurred: the impressionists used these new, scarcely tested colours and their paintings were ruined. Many of them now have patches, imperfect colours, white areas which have become almost yellow, blues which have come to resemble greens, darkened browns or siennas and so on.

But we must not harp on this too much: we must not say, as some famous writers on painting still do, that to avoid such disappointments we should go back to the former manual system of the old masters and make our own oil-paints.

I must make this clear once and for all: we should leave this task to the modern and nowadays skilled manufacturers who experiment with, discover and produce our oil-paints and who have much more knowledge of the subject than we, using much better methods and ingredients than the earlier «kitchen». Let us have no more discussion on this matter (and I would like to include in this the question of printing or preparing canvases, papers and boards for oil-painting since it is not advisable to prepare these at home when you can obtain surfaces which have been prepared and guaranteed by industrial concerns and laboratories). Maurice Bousset wrote in 1927: «The new colours are superior to the old» and after praising the beauty of the range of cadmium yellows, added:

«If Rubens had had such a range available, we should now be able to see his canvases with their original freshness, since the vivid yellows he used have now entirely evaporated».

This is how the dilemma is solved: go to the shop, ask for a good brand of oil colours —yes, a good brand, it doesn't cost a fortune— and paint. Don't bother about anything except painting.

COLOURS, EQUIPMENT AND UTENSILS
FOR OIL-PAINTING

BUYING OIL-PAINTS

«Do you sell oil-colours?»

You have gone into a good shop for artists' materials. The salesman answers: «Which brand would you like? What size tube... large, medium?»

This is what you need to know in order to reply and buy your materials with a good idea of what you require:

BRANDS. You can buy the following brands without any doubts as to their quality: Pelikan, Academie, Schmincker, Reeves, Lefranc, Winsor and Newton, Grumbacher. The artist's own taste will determine which brand he prefers for any particular colour, or for their impasto qualities, etc. Even professional artists commonly use one brand for every colour, with perhaps one or two of a different make.

ASSORTMENT OF COLOURS. Large shops have colour charts supplied by the manufacturers themselves. The charts usually cover a wide range of up to 75 to 90 colours. Professor Max Doerner, the author of one of the major books on artists' materials, was right when he complained about these «long, confusing lists of colours». To show what I mean, I would like to quote the following list of yellows from a North American colour chart: «Lemon yellow, lemon cadmium yellow, light cadmium yellow, medium cadmium yellow, dark cadmium yellow, zinc yellow, cobalt yellow, Naples yellow, reddish Naples yellow, light chrome yellow, medium chrome yellow, dark chrome yellow...».

You must be clear on this point and remember, first of all, that few, if any, of the highly-esteemed contemporary or earlier painters used more than ten or twelve colours at the most, plus white and black. These ten or twelve colours included —and indeed, had to include— the three primaries: yellow, red and blue or, more precisely, medium cadmium yellow, dark madder lake and dark cobalt blue (or Prussian blue). In addition there would have to be an ochre, some sienna, a red, a green, another blue and... but that's *enough!* The final list would include the following colours which we consider to be those most commonly used by professional artists:

COLOURS COMMONLY USED BY PROFESSIONAL ARTISTS

   Lemon cadmium yellow   * *Medium cadmium red*
* *Medium cadmium yellow*   * *Dark madder lake*
* *Yellow ochre*   * *Viridian*
   Raw sienna   * *Dark cobalt blue*
   Burnt sienna   * *Dark ultramarine blue*
   Burnt umber   * *Prussian blue*

* *Titanium white*
  Ivory black

Twelve in all, plus white and black. Notice that nine of these twelve are marked with an asterisk, meaning that they are the most important or, which comes to the same thing, that the other three can be omitted. You will see that white is one of the essential colours while black can be omitted and in fact is the least necessary since it can be made up by mixing Prussian blue, madder lake and green, or Prussian blue, madder lake and burnt umber, etc.

FORM IN WHICH THEY ARE BOUGHT. Oil colours are sold only in tin tubes with a screw-top. Each brand sells four or five different-sized tubes.

As a guide, we give below a table of the sizes available for Titian oil-colours:

CHART OF THE SIZES AND CAPACITIES OF OIL-PAINT TUBES

No. 3	8 cc.
No. 8	21 cc.
No. 14	37 cc.
No. 20	56 cc.
No. 40	122 cc.

When buying colours, you should remember that you must always ask for a larger amount of white since, as we have said, this is the colour most used. According to the above chart, a range of No. 8 tubes will require at least a No. 14 and, better still, a No. 20 tube of white.

Oil-colours are expensive. If a tube is left unsealed or not properly sealed, the paint can be ruined, since it thickens or even becomes dry and hard in the tube and this is impossible to remedy. Do not forget to put the caps back on your tubes when the session is finished.

Finally, some advice upon a difficulty you may encounter. Sometimes the cap of the tube becomes stuck to the screw-top, either because it has been left for several days between sessions or because that particular tube is seldom used. If this happens, do not try to unscrew the cap by force, which may break the tube. Simply light a match and hold the cap over the flame: when the cap is hot, it can be unscrewed easily but use a rag so as not to burn your fingers.

BRUSHES FOR OIL-PAINTING

«Please let me have two or three brushes for oil-painting.»

If you are not more precise, the salesman will show you a number of very large boxes divided into compartments which hold numbered brushes. The brushes will be made of hog's bristles and each case will hold different shapes: in one the brushes will be round, in another flat and so on.

The brushes most commonly used for oil-painting are called «hog brushes» but for special areas, sable brushes are also used. The hog's bristles are the firmest and strongest and thus produce more expressive strokes in most of which it is even possible to see the furrows left by the pressure of the bristles. They are essential for backgrounds and broad areas, and for stumping and shading, irrespective of the size of the area. Sable brushes are more suitable for a smoother style where the coats are even and flat. They are also needed for drawing in outlines and colouring small shapes or details as well as fine lines, etc. For instance, after painting the lips in an oil portrait with a bristle brush, you should use a sable brush with a good round point for adding the fine lines in the flesh and the gap between the lips: it would also be essential for making dark lines in the eye to represent eyelashes, etc.

Both bristle and sable oil-paint brushes are made in three different shapes:

     a) *round*
     b) *flat*
     c) *«bright»*

The figure below gives a full-scale illustration of three brushes of each of these types.

The round brushes are generally used for painting lines. The flat brushes are probably used most since they can be used flat with broad strokes or on edge, producing lines and outlines. This is also true of the «bright» brushes even though, in my personal opinion, they seem to be more suitable for a smoother style of painting, more rounded or curved in keeping with its «cat's tongue» shape. I buy sable brushes with a round tip.

Bristle brushes for oil-painting: from left to right: round, bound with a thread to keep the tip firm; flat (the central three); «bright».

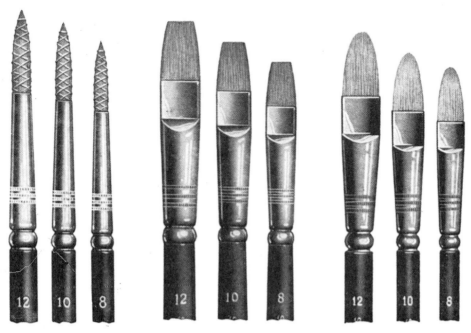

As you know, a brush consists of a handle, ferrule and bunch of bristles: the ferrule is the metal part which encloses the bristles and attaches them to the handle. On oil-painting brushes, the handle is longer than for watercolours. Its length varies between 8 and 9½ inches. This greater length is due to the fact that when we paint in oils, we usually work on a practically vertical surface and nearly always standing some distance from it since we want to see not only the area being painted but the entire surrounding surface. The long handle which enables us to hold the brush at a point further from the bristles, makes it easier for us to stand in that position and have a broader view. The total length of an oil-paint brush, including bristles, ferrule and handle, is between 10¼ and 11¾ inches.

The thickness of the bunch of bristles and, in fact, the entire brush varies according to the number on the handle. These numbers run from 1 to 22 using the even numbers (1, 2, 4, 6, 8, 10, etc.). The figure below gives a full-scale illustration of the complete range of flat brushes.

Obviously, you do not need such an extensive range: it is advisable, however, to have two or more brushes of the same number. This is what we consider a common assortment:

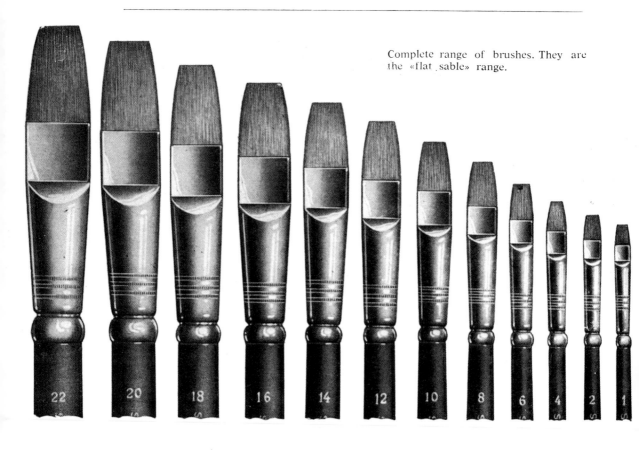

Complete range of brushes. They are the «flat sable» range.

BRUSHES COMMONLY USED BY A PROFESSIONAL ARTIST

a) SMALL ASSORTMENT :

> *1 round hog, No. 4*
> *1 round sable, No. 4*
> *1 flat hog, No. 4*
> *1 flat hog, No. 6*
> *1 «bright» hog, No. 8*
> *1 flat hog, No. 12*

b) LARGE ASSORTMENT :

> *2 round hog, No. 4*
> *2 round sable, No. 4*
> *1 round sable, No. 6*
> *2 flat hog, No. 4*
> *2 flat hog, No. 6*
> *1 flat hog, No. 8*
> *1 «bright» hog, No. 8*
> *2 flat hog, No. 12*
> *1 flat (or «bright») hog, No. 14*
> *1 flat hog, No. 20*

CARE OF BRUSHES

Brushes too are expensive. When you have bought them you must take care of them, not just because of how much they cost, but also because when a brush has been used and kept in good condition it paints better than when it is new.

The main point is to keep them clean after they have been used so that the bristles retain their shape. This is so important that, even when the brush is new, you can see that the bristles have been oiled with a solution of glue or gum arabic. (If this solution is too thick and the bristles really stick together, they must be dipped in lukewarm water).

Going back to the question of cleaning, no difficulty arises while you are painting. The paint is soft and the brushes are being constantly used on the picture. If the session is broken off overnight, for example, you can start again without cleaning your brushes, but if a day elapses and especially if the picture has been completed and it may be two or more days before you paint again, then you must clean the brushes thoroughly until they are like new.

There are two methods of cleaning:

CLEANING WITH TURPENTINE. First dry the brush with a rag, wiping off any paint left on them. Then dip them in a jar of ordinary turpentine, rub the bristles against the sides of the jar, rinse them, dry them and wipe with a rag, then rinse them again and so on.

There are special jars on the market for washing brushes, with a wire screen about half-way up; you fill the jar with turpentine to just above this screen and then rub the brush against it until it is clean and the sediment of colour removed sinks to the bottom of the jar.

After being cleaned in turpentine, the bristles are rather taut (especially in the case of brushes made from young hogs) and are inclined to separate, rather like the old twig-brooms. To prevent this, you can wash the brushes with soap and water after they have been cleaned in turpentine; this leaves the bristles softer and more compact.

CLEANING WITH SOAP AND WATER. This method is very common, firstly because turpentine is not always available (that is to say sufficient amounts of the ordinary type since it would be extravagant to waste refined turpentine, i.e. essence of turpentine, such as that used to dissolve the pigments) and secondly, because it is easier and more pleasant while still giving a more or less perfect wash.

First you clean and wipe off the left-over colour with a rag, removing as much paint as possible. Then, in the bathroom or kitchen, rub the brush on a piece of soap, rather as if you were painting with soap. Wet the brush under the tap and then wash it, rubbing it on the palm of your hand. No matter how inexperienced you are, the soap will immediately produce thick suds tinted with the colour from the brush. Rinse it with water and again apply it to the soap tablet, loading your brush with soap; wash it once more by rubbing it in your palm, rinse it again and so on. Each time the soap-suds will be cleaner until they become completely white. One last rinse under the tap and you've finished.

If you are inexperienced, the only danger with this method is that when you rub the bristles in your palm, you may make them lose their shape by bending them. To prevent this, you must be careful to rub *as if you were painting*, i.e. by resting the head of the brush on your palm and making small circular movement, but always dragging the bristle behind the ferrule. If you do this, you can safely rub them as hard as you like. Try it — it is not difficult.

Finally, when washing either with turpentine or soap, once the brush is clean you must dry it carefully, remembering that if it remains damp, the ends of the bristles held by the ferrule can become unstuck. But that's natural, isn't it? Then leave the brushes in a jar with the bristles and ferrule upwards. This is the usual and decorative way of keeping them in the studio when you are not painting.

SPATULAS

A spatula is a kind of knife with a wooden handle and a blade of flexible steel without a cutting edge. It can be blunt or pointed as well as trowel-shaped, except that the blade is narrower. (See figure below).

In oil-painting, spatulas are used for two main purposes: firstly to scrape the surface when the paint is still soft in order to clean an area, that is for «rubbing out» or correcting, and to clean the left-over paint off the palette when the session is over, and, for painting, using the spatula instead of a brush.

For scraping the surface or the palette, the knife-shaped spatulas are best; with the thinner end — if it is to be used for correcting and «rubbing out» — and a flexible blade; a firmer blade is preferable for cleaning the palette,

When used for painting, flexible spatulas are required and the trowel-shaped ones are commonly used.

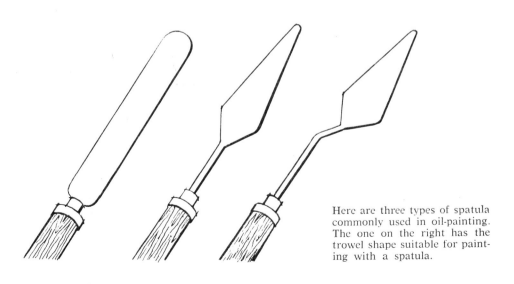

Here are three types of spatula commonly used in oil-painting. The one on the right has the trowel shape suitable for painting with a spatula.

SURFACES FOR OIL-PAINTING

The customary surfaces or supports for oil-painting are: canvas, panels, pasteboard and paper.

CANVASES: These are the most common support due to their elasticity, light weight and flexibility.

Good fabrics for oil-painting are linen and hemp whose corrugation varies according to the warp and thickness of the threads: there are fine, medium and large-grained canvases. The fine-grained ones require a more delicate style while the large-grained surfaces call for a more impressionistic handling and so the medium-grained canvases are used most.

Like pasteboard and panels for oil-painting, canvases are sold primed or prepared, which provides better cohesion and permanence of the colours. This priming, which is applied only to one surface, consists of a coat of glue mixed with distemper or plaster, and is usually white. However, some canvases and other supports are primed with a coloured mixture producing a smooth coat of colour which may be neutral grey, bluish grey or reddish sienna. The choice of a ready-prepared coloured undersurface, such as these greys or sienna, is dictated by the artist's taste and preferences and many old masters painted on canvases which had already been colour-primed. For example, Rubens painted on grey and Velasquez on reddish sienna.

The canvas can be bought mounted on a stretcher or as unmounted pieces which are sold by the yard. Unmounted canvases are usually 28 to 60 inches wide and are suitable for painting murals or simply for fitting on an old stretcher. A stretcher is a wooden frame with small wooden wedges on the inside angles of the corners and when tapped with a hammer, these enable the canvas mounted on the stretcher to be tightened or slackened. The canvas is fixed to the stretcher with just a few small nails.

Like pasteboard and panels, the mounted canvases are classified by numbers according to the size and by a subject description which specifies the picture's final proportion. These descriptions correspond to the following three subjects: *figure, landscape, marine*. The stretchers or pictures classified as «figure» are squarer than «landscape» and «marine» canvases have the greatest width in relation to their height. This classification is to some extent governed by the fact that when painting a seascape, you generally require an area or rectangle whose width and height are more disproportionate than in the case of a surface for a figure or portrait. However, in practice, an artist is not compelled slavishly to abide by these classifications: some paint landscapes on «figure» canvases, and vice versa.

There is an international table of measurements with which every manufacturer of mounted canvases must comply, so when the artist knows this table and has fixed the approximate size of the picture, he chooses one of the sizes from the table and in the shop simply asks for «a figure (landscape or marine) stretcher, number so-and-so».

Here is the table:

INTERNATIONAL SIZES OF OIL-PAINTING STRETCHERS
(cms)

No.	Figure	Landscape	Marine
1	22 × 16	22 × 14	22 × 12
2	24 × 19	24 × 16	24 × 14
3	27 × 22	27 × 19	27 × 16
4	33 × 24	33 × 22	33 × 19
5	35 × 27	35 × 24	35 × 22
6	41 × 33	41 × 27	41 × 24
8	46 × 38	46 × 33	46 × 27
10	55 × 46	55 × 38	55 × 33
12	61 × 50	61 × 46	61 × 38
15	65 × 54	65 × 50	65 × 46
20	73 × 60	73 × 54	73 × 50
25	81 × 65	81 × 60	81 × 54
30	92 × 73	92 × 65	92 × 60
40	100 × 81	100 × 73	100 × 65
50	116 × 89	116 × 81	116 × 73
60	130 × 97	130 × 89	130 × 81
80	146 × 114	146 × 97	146 × 89
100	162 × 130	162 × 114	162 × 97
120	195 × 130	195 × 114	195 × 97

PANELS. These are the wooden panels commonly used as supports by the pre-Renaissance painters. At that period panels required special construction and preparation, but now modern thin ply-wood or pressed wood panels provide the artist with permanent, light-weight rigid supports. In this respect the «Tablex» wood prepared with a coat of gum and plaster is the best, since it offers a smooth matt surface which is very suitable for preliminary trials and small subjects. It is available in sizes up to Nos. 6 and 8 of the above list.

A plywood panel, some 3/16" thick, with an ordinary coat of size or carpenter's glue which must be very liquid, is also suitable for painting and you can prepare this yourself.

CARDBOARD. This is used for painting preliminary sketches and small pictures. You can buy prepared cardboard with white, smooth matt priming.

Like wood, cardboard can be prepared at home simply by applying a coat of size, but make sure that you coat both sides to prevent the moisture from warping the cardboard.

Providing it is of good quality, thick and well-pressed, modern grey cardboard can be used with no preparation except a coat of oil-paint from the tube after it has been thinned with essence of turpentine. This removes some of the absorbent quality of cardboard. The coat must be completely dry before you start to paint.

PAPER. Surprising as it may seem, paper is also an excellent support for oil-painting. Rubens and other old masters used it for drafts and sketches and it was also used by the impressionists for painting preliminary sketches which were then worked up into finished pictures.

The essential condition is that the paper must be thick and of very good quality, well-primed, etc., that is to say paper such as the Canson brand or fine-grained watercolour paper. No preparation is required and you can therefore paint directly onto it. Since it is so fragile and liable to contract and expand, it is not, of course, advisable to paint finished works and, even less, large pictures. However, it is excellent for studies, sketches and rough notes.

THE PALETTE

«Whichever you like,» says the salesman, «we stock round and rect-angular palettes in wood, china and plastic.»

And he shows them to you. Every type has an elliptical hole at one end with bevelled edges, perfectly shaped for the thumb of the left hand. Near this hole there is also a kind of indentation which is shaped and positioned in such a way that the palette can be held by the index and middle fingers.

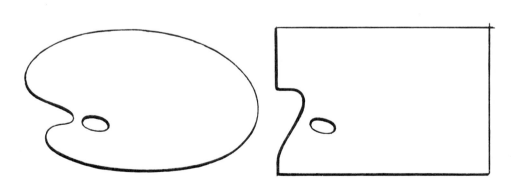

Traditional palettes for oil-painting: oval and rectangular.

Hold a palette, test it, feel it in your hand resting on your forearm... and ask yourself:

«Oval or rectangular?»

It is a matter of taste. In the studio, the oval palette seems more suitable — and more artistic — but, when painting out of doors, the box palette is used and that is rectangular... perhaps it is less attractive, cruder. It is, as I have said, just a matter of taste.

Wood, china or plastic?

Definitely wood! Like most artists, I feel that a china or plastic palette, especially the latter, is out of place in an artist's studio.

What size?

Every painter keeps at least two and usually three palettes in his studio. All are of different sizes: a small one, which he uses for notes, sketches and small pictures; one medium-sized and one large, which is kept for large pictures. So the answer to this question is that the size corresponds to the size of the picture being painted. Needless to say, the larger the palette, the more space it contains and so the more convenient and functional it is.

The palette must be cleaned when the work is finished. Some colour may be left in it and, if so, when you begin a new painting the next day or the day after, you may find these left-overs useful. Nevertheless, it is nearly always best to start again from scratch and clean the palette thoroughly so that you can begin with fresh colour straight from the tube. Use newspaper first and then rub the palette with old rags and finally with a rag slightly moistened with turpentine.

SOLVENTS

Oil-paint straight from the tube is nearly always too thick for painting properly. To dilute it for applying coats, etc. the artist uses what are called «mediums», which are liquid solvents suitable for thinning the paints.

ESSENCE OF TURPENTINE. This is the best solvent. As we have already said, it dries quickly through evaporation and so when mixed with oil-colours, no matter how oily, it accelerates the drying process and makes it easier to superimpose further coats, especially when painting notes or pictures which have to be completed in one or two sessions.

Essence of turpentine gives colours a matt quality which is highly-esteemed by some contemporary painters.

However, only very small amounts must be used, both to avoid excessive liquefaction of the colour and in order not to destroy the adhesive quality of the paint, i.e. the density required to stick to the surface or support.

LINSEED OIL. This is another commonly used solvent, but it is rarely employed unmixed and, of course, oil-colour straight from the tube already contains a considerable quantity of linseed oil. If it is diluted with yet more oil, the resulting mixture becomes even more greasy, which obviously delays drying. In principle, this does not involve any danger from the point of view of technique and for some subjects and techniques it can even be an advantage, making it possible to paint over comparatively soft coats applied at the previous session.

When the picture is completed, linseed oil used as a solvent produces the traditional shiny surface of oil-paintings. However, this shine may be uneven since some colours dry more rapidly than others. To solve this problem, it is best to varnish the picture when it is finished and dry.

MIXED SOLUTION (ESSENCE OF TURPENTINE AND LINSEED OIL). The above explanations have implied that one of the classic solvents for oil-paints is a mixed solution consisting of essence of turpentine and linseed oil. In every case the proportion used in this mixture is governed by (a) the subject, which may require rapid or slow work; (b) the support's absorption capacity and: (c) the finish, which may be shiny or matt.

DRYERS. These are also used as solvents for accelerating the drying process. They can be bought made-up in jars from shops specialising in artist's materials. It is advisable to use them only in special cases.

Finally, we can say that generally speaking solvents must be added only in very small amounts since in most cases the oil-paint from the tube already has the perfect consistency for painting without any necessary addition.

OIL JARS

These are small containers for the solvents — essence of turpentine and linseed oil. The classic model consists of two small metal cans with a kind of catch at the base by which they can be attached to the palette. When working in the studio, it is common practice to use any container providing it is small and shallow: a shallow glass with a wide mouth, a china or porcelain jar such as a piece from a toy dinner service, an ash-tray, etc.

RAGS

Lots of these. A lot of rags are required for oil-painting. They are used for drying brushes, especially for cleaning them when changing from one colour to another, and also for rubbing out on the canvas, for cleaning the palette, etc. Any type will do provided they are old.

STUDIO EASEL

When working at home or in the studio, it is perfectly all right to use an outdoor easel, that is to say a folding easel as used for painting out of doors. But professional artists usually have at least one studio easel on which it is easier and safer to work.

The figure overleaf shows three types of studio easel: the first (A) has a simple but traditional frame and is commonly used in art schools. Notice that the shelf for holding the canvas (*a*) can be raised at will in keeping with the size of the picture by using the toothed bar set in the central support (*b*). This is the cheapest of the three.

The second (B) is probably the most popular for professional studios. This type is very solid and firm due to its design and structure: it can be moved easily on the set of four castors: the shelf for the canvas can be raised or lowered and an attachment (*c*) which is also adjustable can be fixed to the central support to hold the canvas or stretcher at the top.

Finally type (C) is a de luxe model with the following principal features: two shelves for holding small and large pictures; a central support which can be inclined to facilitate work on large canvases; a board, which can also be adjusted at will, for drawing and painting small sketches, miniatures, drafts, etc. Needless to say, this is the most expensive model.

...AND AN EXTRA PIECE OF FURNITURE

We are still in your studio at home. When you start painting as an amateur you need only arrange and keep your tubes of paint, jars of solvents, oil jars, spatulas, etc. in a box similar to those used for painting out of doors. But later — or now if you want to set up a proper studio — you should consider obtaining a rather small table (which can have castors so that you can move it easily) with a washable top (formica, for example) and enough drawers for storing your tubes, brushes, jars, etc. In my opinion, it is best to explain your requirements to a carpenter and draw a sketch of it yourself: remember that the most convenient height is about 24 to 28 inches, no more.

VARIOUS MATERIALS

You will also need a black crayon, pencils, a drawing-board for when you paint on a small sheet of paper or cardboard, drawing-pins, a can or bottle for the turpentine...

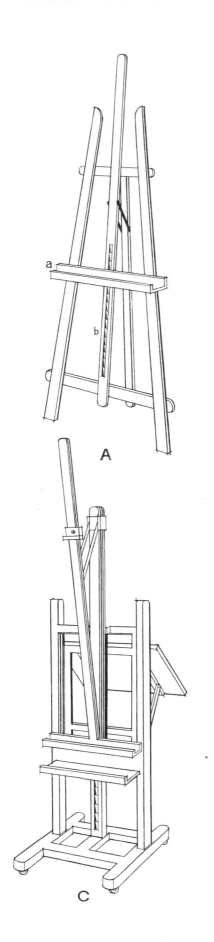

A

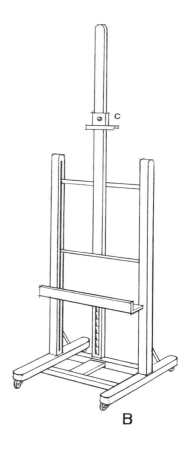

B

C

This page shows three types of easel for studio work. Type A, the simplest of the three, is commonly used in art schools. Type B can be said to be the most commonly used in professional artists' studios. Type C has a number of advantages, the most obvious being the drawingboard at the back which can be sloped at will, for drawing or painting small pictures, miniatures, preliminary sketches, etc.

SPECIAL EQUIPMENT FOR PAINTING IN OILS OUT OF DOORS

The only «special equipment» really needed for painting out of doors is a box for carrying and keeping materials, an outdoor easel and a stool for sitting down when you get the chance.

A BOX FOR OIL-PAINTING

Various sizes are available but in structure they are more or less identical. They are made of wood and contain various compartments for storing the tubes of colours, brushes, spatulas, jars of solvents, oil-jars, rags, etc. Every type also contains a palette adapted for fitting into

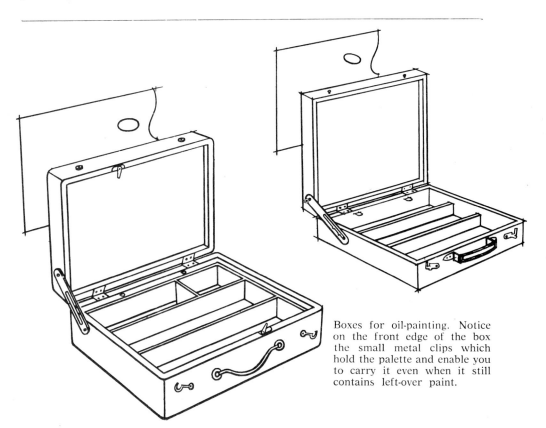

Boxes for oil-painting. Notice on the front edge of the box the small metal clips which hold the palette and enable you to carry it even when it still contains left-over paint.

the box. To enable you to carry the palette without having first to clean it, the box has small metal clips which hold the palette without letting it touch the base of the lid. Some models have similar arrangements for carrying newly-painted cardboard sheets when they are the same size as the inside of the lid.

Apart from this, the quality and price of the boxes are determined not only by the size but also by the construction and finish.

The above illustration shows two of the most common types.

33

OUTDOOR EASELS

These consist basically of a wooden tripod with special arrangements which enable it to be folded up for carrying.

There are several different types but each one must satisfy the following conditions: (*a*) light in weight; (*b*) solid; (*c*) when it is set up, it must be high enough to enable the artist to paint standing if he wishes; (*d*) adjustable height for painting when sitting, standing, etc.; (*e*) it must be possible to fix the picture firmly at the top so that, as far as possible, it is immovable.

This figure below shows two types which satisfy these conditions.

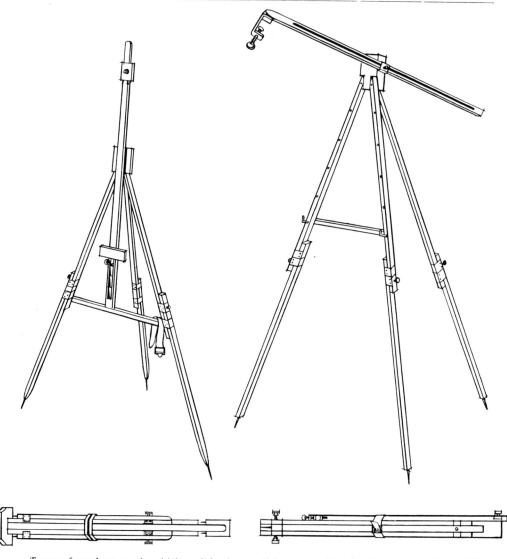

Types of outdoor easels which satisfy the conditions described in the text (weight, solidity and manoeuvrability).

COMBINED EASEL AND BOX

An easel which embodies the box is distinguished by the number of parts, joints and special arrangements which enable it to be set up and taken down in a minute while still providing a solid and really practical unit.

Look at the figure below and notice, particularly in Type B, the number of adjustments which can be made when it is set up: sloping the picture, holding it by means of the lower shelf and the hooks at the top which after adjustment, are suitable for a small sketch or a large picture; the possibility of lowering or raising the whole unit by sliding the legs, etc. Notice too that when it is folded, it is even smaller than the ordinary box. A pity it's so expensive...

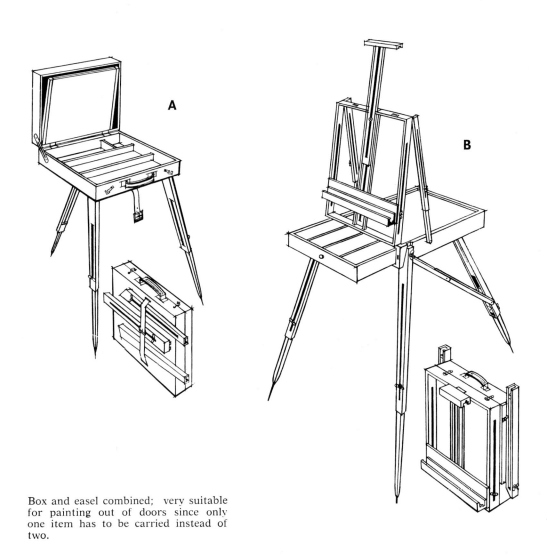

A

B

Box and easel combined; very suitable for painting out of doors since only one item has to be carried instead of two.

«HAVE YOU ANY STOOLS?»

«Yes, sir. A stool is always a good idea for taking a rest» says the salesman, looking as if he could do with one himself. Then he tries them, testing which are firm and demonstrating «with complete frankness» which of them are satisfactory.

You look at them... but wait: don't buy one yet. If you are lucky enough to have a car or if you don't bother about carrying a pound or two more, instead of one of these stools, I would advise you to buy a folding metal chair of the type which are now made for camping: they are firm, light and much more comfortable. I warn you that this is rather important: in an intellectual job like painting, physical comfort influences the final results.

«Do I need to look at or know anything else?» you ask.

«No, I don't think so. But wait a moment: you haven't got a stretcher carrier.»

STRETCHER-CARRIERS

These are a simple but essential item for carrying a newly-painted picture. They consist of two parts: firstly, a handle fixed to a metal clasp in the centre of which is attached a metal strip. Each end of the

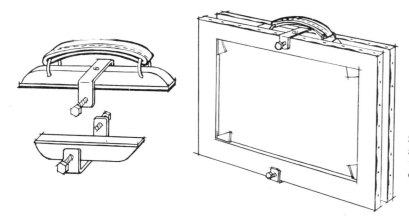

Stretcher-carriers. These enable you to carry a newly painted picture without risk of damage.

metal clasp has a screw so that two canvases or stretchers can be fixed each side of the strip.

Secondly, a similar clasp, but without the handle, also holds the two canvases apart. So you need another stretcher and canvas of about the same size in order to carry a newly-painted picture. See the figure above.

. . . .

That's all. Nothing more is needed for oil-painting. We still have to study the whys and wherefores of the question, but that will be dealt with in the following pages.

PRACTICE IN OIL-PAINTING

FIRSTLY WITH ONLY TWO COLOURS

We shall follow the traditional method of most art schools. First of all, you will practice and paint with only two colours, or rather with one colour and white: then with three — the primaries, blue, red and yellow; and finally you will use every colour.

We are using this method because we assume that we are starting from scratch and you have never painted in oils before. We take it, therefore, that you know nothing about the fluidity, softness, covering power and drying times of the colours, nor the potential of that softness and opacity by means of which an artist can cover, outline and trim, drawing while he paints. We assume that you are equally unaware of the natural properties of that softness under the influence of an expert brush which shades, models, depicts and paints the forms, producing that synthesis of form which we so much admire in the old masters. We feel that this skill, this introduction to skilful handling, should not be confused with and complicated by the real problem of painting, namely to see and mix the colours.

So, we shall take our first steps with only one colour. This is a traditional approach, as I have said, but we introduce one new factor: in this initial stage, it is usual to paint with black and white but we shall use white and a very dark sienna, burnt umber which is almost as dark as black but is pleasanter, warmer and even more chromatic: at all events, it is nicer to work with than a cold, monotonous black.

Using only these two colours our first practical exercise will be to paint a cube, a sphere and a jug but without working from a model: this initial stage will enable us to test the medium and also, incidentally, to see how the palette is used, how the brushes are held, how to paint with brushes and so on.

Later you will advance to three colours, the three primaries, discovering — and learning — that every colour in nature can be made up from just these three.

Finally, when you have the skill and know all about colours... —that's just a manner of speaking since the more you know, the more you realise how much more there is to know— then you will get down to painting with every colour commonly used by the professional artist. We shall then go on to a practical study of subjects.

That is the broad outline of our plan. Let's start on the first stage right away:

GENERAL INSTRUCTIONS

MATERIALS REQUIRED FOR THESE EXERCISES

Oil-paints	Titanium white
	Burnt umber
Brushes (hog)	«Bright» No. 8
	Flat, No. 4
	Round, No. 4
Sable brushes	Round, No. 8 (or 10)
Palette	
Solvents	Essence of turpentine
	Linseed oil
Oil-jars (or a small container)	
Support	Thick Canson paper and cardboard
Rags, drawing-pins, pencil	

We have not mentioned the easel since we assume you have that. But don't worry if you have not got one for these early exercises or «homework». For the time being, you can simply use a chair, resting a drawing-board on the seat and leaning it against the back: fix the Canson paper or cardboard to it with drawing-pins as shown in the figure.

1. TAKE THE PALETTE, BRUSHES AND A RAG

See how the palette, brushes and rag are held in these illustrations: all in the left hand, leaving the right free for painting. Remember this (and try it while examining these pictures).

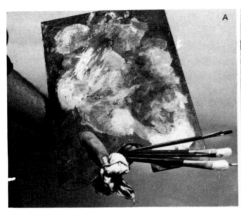

The palette is held mainly by the thumb which, either by itself or with the help of the other fingers in the shape of a clasp, can keep it at a slightly oblique angle and away from the forearm (A) or horizontally, resting it on the forearm which helps to take the weight (B).

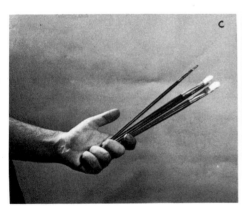
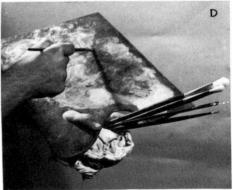

In the next figure (C) notice how the brushes are held to form a fan-shape so that the paint on one does not rub off on the others. Notice in figure (D) how the artist holds the palette, brushes and rag in his left hand.

The method shown in (D) is the usual way of painting out of doors. When working in the studio, some artists prefer to place the palette on a chair or small table in front of or beside the easel. This method is preferred due to the weight of a large palette which can be tiring for a session lasting an hour or an hour and a half. With this system, only the brushes are held in the left hand and the rag is placed on the table beside the palette.

2. ARRANGING THE COLOURS

Take the tubes of white and burnt umber. Squeeze out some of both, placing the white on the top right-hand side and the burnt umber beside it. Remember that at the beginning, there should be about twice as much white as umber.

We should mention in passing that, when he is working with all the colours, an artist sets them out on his palette in a specific order, following the general rule of the lightest on the right, headed by white, and the darker paints to the left;   they are placed around the edge of the palette so that the centre is left for mixing. The figure below shows how I arrange my own palette.

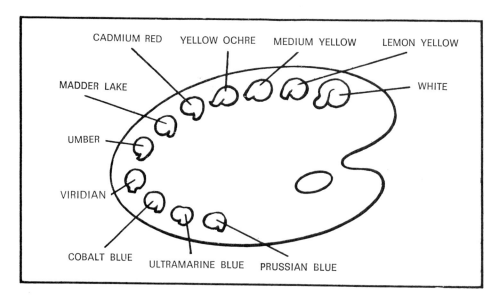

3. WHERE TO HOLD THE BRUSH

As we said earlier, brushes for oil-painting are produced with longer handles than those for watercolours or other techniques. This is because they have to be held at the tip or two-thirds of the length away from the bristles, as you can see in the illustrations opposite. This is due to the distance which the artist must keep from the picture when he is painting. When working on a standard sized surface or even on stretcher sizes Nos. 1 and 2, the artist never paints on top of the picture, as it were, as in the case of watercolours or drawing. Let me emphasise this important rule :

Oil-painting requires a certain distance between the artist and the picture. This can be 3 feet or more depending upon the size of the picture.

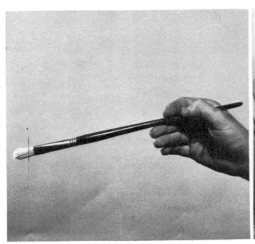

To cover this distance, the artist stretches his arm and holds the brush by the further end of the handle.

«But why?» you ask. Well, there are many reasons: because, more than any other technique, oil-painting requires that the artist has a full view of the picture all the time; so that he can see it and paint it simultaneously, moving from area to area without being held up at any particular point. Also because this distance induces a smoother, more pleasant and more impressionistic technique. You will see for yourself, for instance, that when you hold the brush by the upper end, the range of the head is much greater than if you hold it by the ferrule as you do with a pencil: you will realise that this wider range encourages broad strokes, a spontaneous touch in the modern, impressionistic style.

You may think that in Van Eyck's pictures, for example, the careful detailed manner in which the shapes were painted are inconsistent with this method of working and holding the brush. I agree; he used a different style. In his period most pictures were painted on a desk with the canvas or panel slightly sloped, and the brush was held like a pencil or pen. But study the handling of Rubens or Velázquez (when it was common practice to use an easel with the canvas in a vertical position) and you will see sections in which the synthesis is exactly the same as that found in the Impressionists at the end of the last century: you will realise that for this style it was necessary to paint from a distance and to hold the brush by the tip or upper part of the handle.

This does not mean that on occasion the hand is not moved down to the ferrule. This is particularly true in the case of figure studies or portraits when you have to paint in the light in an eye, the exact shape of a nostril, the line between the lips, etc. We shall discuss these «unorthodox» brush-strokes later but you must understand that for these minute touches an artist uses the maulstick, a long stick tipped with a ball wrapped in a piece of cloth.

4. HOW TO HOLD THE BRUSH

We have seen *where* to hold the brush — at the top or clasp, — and now we shall see *how* to hold it by examining the advantages offered by each of the two common ways of holding the brush: the normal way and with the handle along the palm.

HOLDING THE BRUSH IN THE NORMAL WAY

«In the normal way» means like a pencil or pen for writing but higher up. However, there are two alternatives: (*a*) the ordinary way, and (*b*) keeping the brush in the same position but giving the hand a quarter-turn.

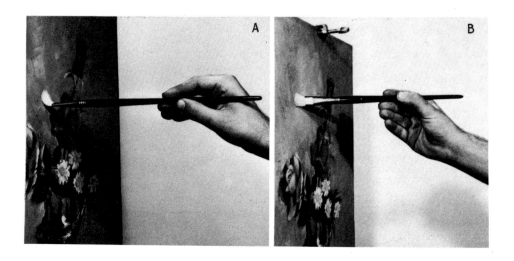

Hold the brush yourself and try both positions so that you can understand better when I say that:

In position A (normal way of holding a pencil) you can paint in every direction, upwards and downwards, using vertical or diagonal strokes. You can also paint horizontally simply by revolving the brush from left to right or vice versa.

Notice too that with A, the brush is virtually perpendicular to the surface of the canvas or cardboard; in other words, the brush and surface form a right angle. This is an important detail which strongly affects the type of stroke.

Genuinely *put these instructions into practice: use a hog brush No. 8 or 10, applying colour and really painting on Canson paper or cardboard.*

In this position, the tip rather than the body of the brush is applying the colour. If you want to paint a dot, a thin line, a bright spot, etc. you need only apply the brush to the right area, but if you want to make a broad stroke, you must use pressure and bend the bristles, which makes the stroke firmer, harder and more clearly defined, stronger, in fact.

When using position B, on the other hand, the brush remains slightly at an angle to the surface when the hand turns a few degrees. The stroke is flatter; the bristles offer less resistance and, as they do not have to bend as did before, they form a right angle: thus, if he wishes, the artist can paint more smoothly and less forcefully.

HOLDING THE BRUSH WITH THE HANDLE ALONG THE PALM

This automatically means that the brush has to be held closer to the bristles, more or less in the middle of the handle. It produces and entails a broad, very free style, unsuitable for small details.

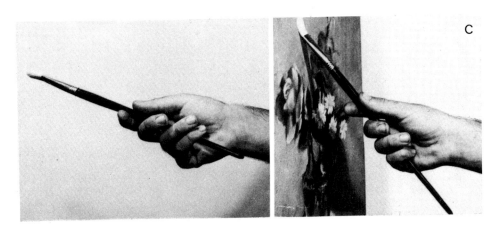

C

Notice that if you hold the brush in this way, it forms a much smaller angle with the surface, moving towards the horizontal position. The tip of the brush can even paint lying flat along the surface. The stroke is not governed by the bent bristles as it is in the earlier position. On the contrary, we could say that rather than making strokes, we *place* the brush on the surface, *depositing* colour.

WHY AN ARTIST MUST MASTER THESE THREE WAYS OF HOLDING THE BRUSH

Simply because each way produces different effects. You will already have realised that:

Using method A with the tip of the brush touching the surface, you can paint and mix colours, working on an area which is still wet; you can apply colour by rubbing or scraping the bristles of the brush over a dry surface, using a strong shading movement. This is the best method for shading with a «strong» brush, that is to say by applying the tip, bending the bristles and darting the brush in a quick movement. It is also suitable for applying colour in the pointilliste style and then blending it with the previous coat while it is still wet, and so on. It is also the most suitable method for giving a firm outline to a shape, for painting with strong, firm touches.

Generally speaking, method B produces a smoother stroke. It is also useful and indeed essential for blending and shading on wet areas, for «pointing» and blending, for tinting a colour, putting in outlines... but in every case with less strength and with less effect upon existing colours or forms.

Finally with the handle along the palm, method C, you can apply colour without blending it with previous coats. Suppose, for instance, you want to paint a white line on a dark, still wet area without allowing the wet paint to dirty the white: to caress, deposit and gently place colour upon colour; to soften a hard edge, an over-firm outline with the clean brush...

Yes, indeed, the three methods are in constant use and all three must be learnt and mastered until you automatically and instinctively apply them whenever they are needed. The ideal is not to think of *how* it is done but only of *what* you are doing.

Now, practice makes perfect and so we are going to paint. You can

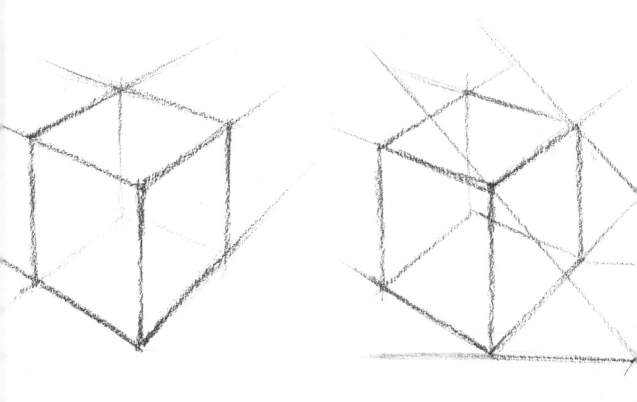

now begin to paint in oils without needing to know anything more. Our first exercise is to paint a cube in oils.

Are you ready? Have you got Canson paper, palette, paints, brushes, rag...?

5. TAKE A GOOD PENCIL AND DRAW A CUBE ON A SEPARATE PIECE OF PAPER

«But I thought you said we were going to paint?»

«So we are, but do you remember what Ingres said: 'paint as you draw'?» That is what we are doing. If you can make a perfect drawing from memory of an oblique view of a cube you can omit this exercise and start painting. But do not later produce a badly done exercise because you haven't really an accurate mental picture of a cube, the shadow it casts and the perspective it entails. Bear in mind that while you are painting the cube, you must be seeing an image of it, noting the position and exact size of each edge, the proportion between the faces, and so on, just as if your painting was a film projection of a perfectly formed and drawn cube: a projection which would enable you to paint and follow the image; AN IMAGE WHICH MUST BE FIRMLY FIXED IN YOUR MIND'S EYE.

Only in this way can you paint a perfect cube.

I am sorry to harp on this point but you should draw the cube on a separate piece of paper, or at least look at the series of drawings below and remember them.

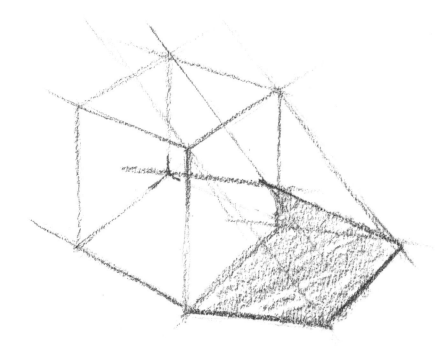

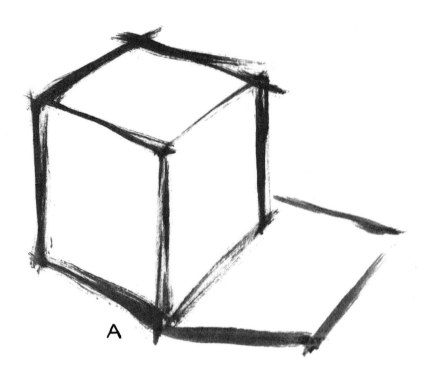

A

6. COMPOSITION (A)

Flat hog brush, no. 4; rag; burnt umber thinned with essence of turpentine.

I. — Be careful with the essence of turpentine. It is by no means a matter of mixing a liquid solution, but simply of wetting the brush in the jar of turpentine and applying it to the paint so that, with the help of this moisture, we will produce a fluid but not runny paint, a paint which runs and which can be used for drawing lines.

II. — As you can see in Figure A, you have to make an outline sketch of a cube in two dimensions, without following any preliminary pencil lines but simply drawing directly on the white paper with a brush and the burnt umber.

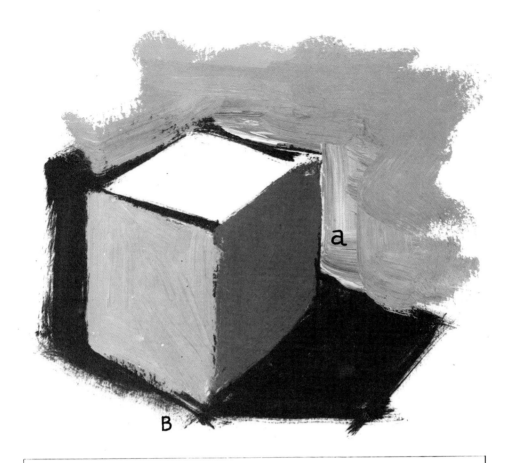

7. FIRST STAGE (B)

Flat hog brush, no. 4; round brush, no. 4; and «bright» brush, no. 8; rag; burnt umber and white.

(Refer to Figure B while you read these instructions).

I. — Using the same no. 4 flat brush and the burnt umber, which must be pasty and undiluted, paint the dark area of the shadow cast by the cube.

II. — Still using the same colour, paint the dark patch surrounding the illuminated face of the cube.

III. — With the same brush, paint the lateral face of the cube after adding some white to the burnt umber.

IV. — Now take the no. 8 brush, mix the light sienna of the front face of the cube and paint it. Use plenty of paint and apply it thickly.

V. — Now darken the background. Use the no. 8 brush and take a touch of sienna, but rather darker than the previous tone; paint with strong strokes. By mixing a little white on the surface itself, lighten the area bordering the shadow behind the cube (marked «a»).

THICK OR THIN PAINT?

In principle I would say a thick, impasto paint, which shows the material and the strokes. This conforms with the modern style.

The thickness is, of course, dependent upon the amount of solvents used, whether essence of turpetine or linseed oil. (Remember that essence of turpentine is also called white spirit and I shall use this term from now on since it is shorter).

How much white spirit should be mixed with the pigments to produce a thick, paste-like paint?

It depends, of course. But, generally speaking, a very small amount, about as much as is picked up by the brush when the tip is dipped in the white spirit: sometimes, even less than that, when the paint from the tube is already oily and not very thick.

To give a firm rule:

To produce a modern finish with thick paint, use very small amounts of solvent and even none at all, especially when the paints from the tube are already fluid and oily.

PAINT FEARLESSLY

Try to use a lot of colour and thick paint, especially in the lighter areas. Work carefully and attentively, calculating and studying each step, but as boldly and strongly as you can. When you are actually painting, work rapidly, freely and fluently. Then stop, relax and study what you have done. Examine your work carefully and take your time in working out what you must do next. Then start again with enthusiasm and paint bravely and boldly.

ONE BRUSH FOR EACH COLOUR?

Yes, and no.

When using every colour, you generally keep 4, 6 and even 8 brushes in your hand, one or two for the dark colours, two or three for the reds and siennas, another two for the yellows, one for very light colours and white, etc.

THE RAG FOR CLEANING BRUSHES

In any case, whenever you have to mix a new shade or colour, you must clean the brush first with the rag. To make it really clean, you can even dip it in white spirit.

C

8. SECOND STAGE (C)

Flat hog brush, no. 4; round brush, no. 4; «bright», no. 8; rag; burnt umber and white.

I. — Carry on with the background, spreading the greyish medium sienna until you finish it. Use plenty of very thick paint.

II. — When you have finished the background, you will see the reason for the dark patches which you painted in the first stage and which outline the highlight areas of the cube. You will see in fact that the dark colour reminds you how useful it is to contrast and strengthen the border areas so that the lights acquire more power. It also suggests the possibility of leaving a narrow strip of this dark colour as a means of outlining the shape... but without forming that traditional clumsy line which is so often used by an amateur to give shape and outline to the form.

III. — Paint the top lightest surface of the cube, using the no. 4 round brush: this will allow you to go right into the corners.

IV. — Now for the finishing touches: first blend the tones by repainting if necessary. Do not emphasise the outline too much and do not paint with bent bristles (system A) but by sloping and leaning the brush (system B). Use a well-loaded brush so that it produces «dragged» brush-work like that along the edges of the shadow. Whiten the light areas of the background where it joins the shadowed face. Darken the nearest edge of the shadowed lateral face and shade it so that it fades towards the background. Finally, try to give life to the initial dark lines with which you drew the form of the cube.

V. — Examine the direction of the brush-strokes and see whether they bring out the form of the cube without being regular and mathematically precise.

9. PAINTING A SPHERE. COMPOSITION (A)

Flat hog brush, no. 4; rag; burnt umber.

I. — Draw directly with the no. 4 brush and burnt umber as you did with the cube, but dilute the paint with a very small amount of white spirit. Remember that if you use too much white spirit, the paint will run and spread, producing oily patches on the paper. So, I repeat: a very small amount of white spirit.

10. FIRST STAGE (B)

Flat hog brush, no. 4; round brush, no. 4; «bright» brush, no. 8; rag; burnt umber and white.

I. — Still using the no. 4 brush and thick burnt umber, paint the shadow cast by the sphere and the shadow formed on it. For the latter area use an almost dry brush, sketching in the form with the dragged strokes shown in Fig. B.

II. — Now deal with the background, applying white mixed with a very small amount of burnt umber. Work fearlessly with a lot of paint and a well-loaded no. 8 brush.

11. SECOND STAGE (C)

Same materials as before.

I. — Outline the sphere with the no. 8 brush, first using a medium sienna and painting with circular strokes the medium-toned area surrounding the highlight and then blending that greyish medium sienna with the dark

A

B

C

sienna of the shadowed area. Finally, paint the highlight and lightest section of the sphere with white and the no. 4 round brush.

II. — You are now working with one brush for each tone: the no. 4 flat for dark tones the no. 4 round for highlights and light tones and the no. 8 for the intermediate tones. The no. 8 will play the most important part, blending and shading, drawing and outlining.

III. — Back to the background. Do not spend all your time on modelling the sphere until it is perfect! There is nothing worse than concentrating on one area, going over and over it again without paying any attention to the rest. Notice how the background outlines and brings out the shape of the sphere in Figure C.

IV. — Now the finishing touches. Return to the sphere with clean brushes and paint the line of reflected light along the edge of the shadow. Apply pure white in the highlight and very smoothly, without any dragging, work on this highlight until it is blended into the greyish sienna of the intermediate area.

V. — Study the direction of the brush-strokes in Figure C and ensure that the background is not worked in just one way while the strokes on the sphere are circular and ground appears to be formed horizontally.

12. PAINTING A JUG. COMPOSITION (A)

Flat hog brush, no. 4; rag; burnt umber.

PRELIMINARY DRAWING ON A SEPARATE PIECE OF PAPER

I must ask you to make another drawing in soft pencil on a separate piece of paper: this time you must study the jug which is to serve as the last model for these preliminary exercises.

I am asking you to do this so that you can later paint more fluently, having a firm mental image of the structure and form of the model. If you can draw this jug perfectly, you can also paint it perfectly. Shall we try?

How is it going? All right? Does your drawing of the jug have the firmness and assurance of line, the spontaneity of form, the three-dimensional structure and the «apparent simplicity» of this drawing by an expert? Excuse me for setting myself up as an example but is your drawing as good as that shown on this page as a «Final sketch»?

I. — Without following any preliminary pencil lines, sketch in and draw the shape of the jar using the no. 4 flat brush sometimes flat on the paper and sometimes on edge and applying burnt umber slightly diluted with white spirit. Try to produce a true drawing but don't worry if it is slightly misshapen. As long as you know how to draw and are capable of reconstructing by re-drawing in order to produce a final perfect composition, there is no problem.

II. — Notice that here too I have applied dark paint to the background adjoining the well-lit area of the jug.

III. — See too that with the zig-zag strokes (a) applied sparingly I have tried in this very first stage to form the three-dimensional shape by showing the shadowed area on the jug and the reflected light (b).

IV. — Notice also the first stage in producing the cast shadow where I have tried to sketch in the shading and blending.

V. — Finally, you can see how in this first stage, very light tones can be painted with an almost dry brush without any white spirit; this produces light tints by means of dragged brush-work (c).

B

13. SECOND STAGE (B)

Flat hog brush, no. 4; «bright» brush, no. 8; rag; burnt umber and white.

I. — You must work out the values, fix the general tones and rapidly colour the entire picture in order to eliminate the stridency of the white and black and to produce a result which is closer to the tonality of the final stage.

II. — Three, or, at the most, four, tones will be needed for this first step towards the final values. Using the no. 8 brush almost throughout —keeping the flat no. 4 for the darker areas— begin with the light grey of the background and then go on to the other light colour on the jug itself (the highlight). Now immediately deal with the shadowed area of the jug itself and the dark sections along the edges and the interior. Then the dark tone of the table... quickly.

III. — You should not be too concerned with the actual shape of the drawing but neither must you paint so casually as to lose the structure and the initial composition.

14. THIRD STAGE (C)

Three brushes: no. 8, flat; no. 4 round and no. 8 «bright»; rag; burnt umber and white.

I. — Now take a rest. Relax! Ideally, you should leave this stage until later so that you can come back to it with a fresh mind for seeing what you have to do and how you must do it; also after the picture has dried a little, it provides the firm surface required for *re-painting by drawing*. Let's imagine you have now come back to it...

II. — First deal with the jug itself; restructure it by painting and drawing at the same time the forms and tones of the upper half —the edge of the neck, the interior, the varnished patches (i.e. those dark areas around the neck), the handle and its cast shadow. Carefully study the sombre tones and the simplified planes of the model shown in Figure C. Are there three or four tones? No more. Now remember that «going over the line» is not always unimportant but in some cases is even advisable in order to outline the dark-toned areas with lighter tones. There are several instances of this in the upper section of the jug:

— when painting the curve along the upper edge, begin by tinting the entire strip with a dark colour and then go over the line, encroaching on the background so that you can then outline it with the almost white grey colour of the background.

— Using the same dark tone, paint the varnished patches of the shadowed area; then, ignoring the final shape, go over the line so that you can outline it by superimposing the light tone of the jug.

— The same applies to the shadow cast by the handle. Do you see how the light paint «climbs over» the dark, bringing out the shape?

— See again how this method of superimposing light on dark is applied in the nearest section of the top: a white strip is drawn freely with the no. 8 brush, moving from left to right and ending on the right with a flip of the brush which produces the shaded stroke.

III. — Leave this section. Do not add the white highlights which in every picture should be left until last when you are sure that nothing else needs to be retouched. Now work on the body of the jug — the

C

shadowed and the broad well-lit areas. Be careful here. Do not make the mistake of having an over-delicate finish with precise, smooth and old-fashioned shading. It is easy to give way to the pleasure of working the brush to and fro, blending and re-blending... so that you end up with a mechanical picture, cold and lifeless. Here again, paint boldly and rapidly, standing away from the picture: do not pay much attention to precision.

IV. — Now turn to the background. Here you can let yourself go and really enjoy yourself, working with thick paint and a heavily-loaded no. 8 brush... fearlessly.

V. — Finally, examine Figure C and notice the direction of the brush-strokes... good luck... enjoy yourself.

PRACTICAL EXERCISE

We shall continue to use burnt umber and white and acquire practice and skill, but this time painting from nature.

The subject is a still-life.

You must choose the items. You must study and decide upon the composition, that is to say the way in which some objects are placed in relation to others, as well as the viewpoint, light and frame.

There is only one condition: it must be simple. A few objects arranged in the simplest possible manner. You are not trying to «paint a picture» in the true sense of the word but to choose a subject which enables you to paint and practice.

As an example, look at the subject I have chosen and painted for this exercise: a salad cruet, a tomato and an onion. You can use the same subject or change the jars for a stew-pot, mortar, jug, bottle, etc., placing tomatoes, onions, fruit in front of them or at the side.

But don't complicate matters by choosing objects with a difficult shape or by including too many items.

Choose a simple light, the traditional front lateral or ordinary lateral with only one angle and preferably daylight from a door or window. Make the arrangement similar to mine with the vegetables or fruit in the foreground and a middle ground for the object of your choice.

Finally choose a frame in which you can paint the objects on a fairly large scale. Do not make the mistake of most amateurs by making the model too small so that it is lost in the centre of the picture against an over-large background.

These are the only general instructions.

15. PREPARING THE SURFACE

Paint on this cardboard, the ordinary grey material with thickness 22 or 24 and measuring the same as No. 4, Figure stretcher (33 x 24 cm).

You can paint directly on this type of cardboard without any preparation (I know that many artists do so). It has the drawback —or advantage, depending upon which way you look at it— that the spongy fibre quickly absorbs the oil and essences in the paint so that it dries very rapidly and gives a completely matt finish.

To enable us to paint on a more normal surface, we shall carry out a simple preparation as described below:

I. — In a small jar or vase, prepare a solution of:

10 or 12 drops of white spirit
3 or 4 drops of linseed oil
1 portion of white paint
1/3 portion of burnt umber

As you will see, this formula is not precise. We are really trying to produce a greyish light sienna oil paint, diluted with some white spirit and one-third of that amount of linseed oil (very little linseed oil in proportion to the white spirit) so that the paint is thick enough to cover. (To test the thickness, load the brush and hold it in the air to see whether the paint stays on it without dripping). The greyish light sienna must be more or less the same as the background in Figure A below. Add more white or umber until you obtain more or less this tone.

A

B

C

II. — Paint the surface of the cardboard with this solution, using a no. 8 brush. Apply two coats one after the other without waiting for the first to dry.

III. — There you are: you should now wait at least two days for the two washes to be completely dry.

After two days the surface will look matt. The priming or coats of paint will reduce the cardboard's absorption capacity, enabling you to paint under the best possible conditions.

(You can of course do this exercise on prepared cardboard or fabric which is available in the specialist shops. There is no special reason why you need prepare your own cardboard: I have explained this simply to show you how you can prepare your own surface.)

16. COMPOSITION (A)

Flat hog brush, no. 4; rag; burnt umber diluted with a very small amount of white spirit.

PLACING THE SUBJECT

The Figure opposite (A) shows how the subject can be placed in relation to yourself and the light: there should be a maximum of some 7 to 10 feet between you and the subject, forming a triangle with the window or light so that it shines on the subject and the table or stool on which you are painting.

I. — (Look at Figure A.) As before, you must begin by painting and drawing with the flat no. 4 brush and burnt umber, trying to make a two-dimensional sketch of the model. Make this drawing directly on the prepared cardboard without any preliminary pencil sketch.

17. FIRST STAGE (B)

Flat hog brush, no. 4; «bright» brush no. 8; rag; burnt umber and white.

I. — (Look at Figure B). Since you are painting on a medium grey-sienna background, with a few quick strokes of lighter tones you can now fill in the large areas, beginning to harmonize the tones and create contrasts.

Notice this effect on **Figure B**. It is simply a matter of outlining the shapes and trying, incidentally, to obtain more or less the tones shown in the subject.

II. — From the very beginning, use plenty of thick covering paint with scarcely any white spirit.

18. SECOND STAGE (C)

Same materials as before.

I. — Balance the tones. Paint and repaint in an attempt to blend the colouring.

II. — Do not bother too much about the exact shape of the objects, the **precise outline and the position of a line. These will come later. At this** stage, simply study the general tonality and structure and work fairly freely all over the picture since later you will paint over it, emphasize and adjust it in order to obtain the final result.

19. THIRD AND LAST STAGE (D)

Same materials as before as well as a round brush, no. 4 and a sable brush, no. 8 or 10.

This is the last step and at this stage I think it is necessary to *look*, rather than explain. Study and examine the work done between the second and third Figures, B and C, so that you can understand what you have to do and how to do it.

Only one piece of advice:

II. — Synthesize. Try every means of seeing and distinguishing the planes which form the shapes and try to paint them with as few strokes as possible. For instance, look at the oil-jars where I have tried to follow the rule of simplifying and synthesizing the form and colour of the object. To simplify in this way half-close your eyes and block out the lights and shadows, reducing them to flat shapes; then shade with a mere touch of the brush wherever any extra touches are needed.

III. — Finally, paint happily, moving from one side to the other all across the picture; work from a distance, attentively, thoughtfully but boldly...

IV. — Remember: leave the highlights until last.

The following day you may want to add a few touches. Do this... fearlessly. You can see that oil-painting has the advantage that you can always work over it again, go back to it, especially when you are painting for practice with only two colours. When you paint with three colours —the primaries, which is the same as painting with every colour— it is a different matter. Then you... but that belongs to the next chapter. So, I'll leave you for a while to enjoy your exercises.

PAINTING WITH THREE COLOURS

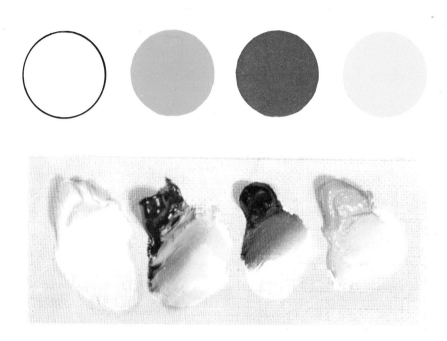

HERE THEY ARE:

From left to right: white, blue, red and yellow.

In oil-colours:

Titanium white
Prussian blue
Dark madder lake
Medium cadmium yellow

If you mix each of these three oil-colours with a little white, you will obtain a blue, purple and yellow which are more or less the same as those reproduced above: a medium, rather greenish blue; a light madder lake, with a purple tinge; a medium, luminous yellow.

This medium blue, madder lake and yellow (the three shown on the top) are the three *primary colours* or the three basic colours which, when inter-mixed, produce the *secondary colours*: green, red and strong blue; then, mixed with the secondaries, they provide the *tertiary colours*: light green, viridian, ultramarine blue, violet, carmine and orange. Every colour in nature, including black (by mixing the three primaries in equal proportions), can be obtained by mixing the three primaries in various proportions.

The three primaries: purple (light carmine), yellow and blue, when inter-mixed, produce the three secondaries: red, green and strong blue. If all the three primaries are superimposed or mixed together, we obtain black (above). In the diagram below we see: the three primaries and the three secondaries mentioned above together with the six tertiaries (light green, viridian, ultramarine blue, violet, carmine and orange), which are obtained by mixing a primary and a secondary.

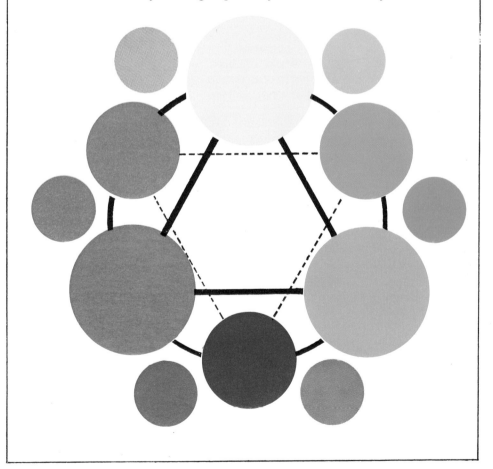

It is worth remembering this:

**All the colours of nature, includ-
ing black, can be obtained from
the three primary colours, blue,
purple and yellow (1).**

Rubens painted with four or, at the most, five colours. Titian painted with an even smaller range and said: « It is possible to be a great painter using only three colours.»

The truth is, however, that it is inconvenient to paint always with just the three primaries: it is impractical to keep trying to mix an ochre for example, from blue, purple and yellow when ochre can be obtained in a tube ready for use and also for mixing with white, blue, purple, etc. in order to provide the exact shade of the model rapidly and easily.

Nevertheless this effort to obtain every colour from only the three primaries is certainly extremely valuable from the point of view of training and leads to a thorough practical knowledge of mixing and obtaining tones, shades and colours; for seeing and capturing the model's colours, you must understand one basic rule:

**Every colour always contains a
proportion of blue, a further
proportion of purple or carmine
and another yellow.**

This applies to flesh-tints, the colour of the earth, the blue sky, green leaves and red flowers. To be accurate, each of these colours must use some measure of the three primaries. Look at your hand and notice its flesh colour. Basically this colour is composed of red, yellow and white, but without blue you would simply obtain a light orange or light cream which is suitable for some special touches and areas —probably the more luminous points— but in no way corresponds to the general colour of the hand. If your skin is tanned, you will need more blue; if it is white, less blue but there will always be some blue, red and yellow. A sky requires a little carmine and yellow which produces a deeper less strident and more realistic blue. Red flowers contain yellow in their highlights and reflections and there is some blue too in the shadowed areas and cast shadows.

You will see this for yourself since we are going to study with practical exercises the potential of the three primaries in oil-painting and the irrefutable fact that the majority, if not all, of the tones and shades contain blue, purple and yellow.

---

(1) The Colour Theory and the potential of the three primaries in oil-painting are discussed in detail in « Painting » which is one of the books in this series. We strongly recommend you to read that book which will help you to understand this one better.

A BASIC PRACTICAL EXERCISE

Before going any further and discussing the materials and preparations, I must tell you that this practical exercise is undoubtedly one of the most important when learning to paint with oils; firstly, because better than any number of instructions it will teach you how to mix colours, what amounts of blue, carmine and yellow are needed for any specific shade, as well as how one colour influences another, how to obtain such vague but common colours as the greys of a dawn, the siennas and golds of an autumn landscape, the blues, greys and purples of a background, an interior or an object in shadow. Secondly, because from this exercise using only three colours you will learn to employ a wider range of colours more knowledgeably in exactly the right proportions.

This exercise will also teach you that you must work with a clean palette and brushes in order to obtain clean colours, that is to say colours which are not impaired by shades left over from earlier mixtures: from it you will obtain practical experience of the varying degrees of opacity, density and intensity of some colours in comparison with others; you will learn to «paste» pigments, and to mix them in the palette or directly over the area already painted, correcting a tone, re-painting over another colour and so on.

Let's begin now without any further introduction:

PAINTING WITH ONLY THREE COLOURS

This is a question of painting 80 different colours using only the three primaries and white.

You can see these 80 colours on the following pages: they are numbered and classified by tones and ranges. You will remember that each of the different colour ranges which can be used for painting a picture can be sub-divided into the warm and cold ranges. You also know that the cold colours contain blue as the dominant basic colour while the warm colours are based upon red.

So the colour chart given on the following pages includes a clear distinction between warm and colour ranges. Notice that in general colours 1 to 40 are predominantly warm tones and colours with yellows, reds, carmines, ochres, siennas, green and even blues have a reddish tinge. On the other hand, colours 41-80 comprise a cold range with greens, blues, purples, ochres and even siennas, all with a bluish tinge and with blue as the dominant note.

Pay special attention to this division into warm and cold when you start to paint and base the mixture upon *carmine* and yellow or upon *blue* and to a lesser extent carmine, according to whether the range is warm or cold.

MATERIALS REQUIRED FOR THESE EXERCISES

Oil paints:
Titanium white
Prussian blue
Dark madder lake
Medium cadmium yellow

Hog brushes:
«Bright» no. 8
Flat, no. 8
Round, no. 4

Palette

Solvents:
White spirit

Oil-jars (or a small container)

Support (surface)
Thick Canson paper

Rags, drawing-pins, pencil

As you can see, you need only three brushes. This is because, when you are learning, you should find out for yourself that your brush has to be cleaned very frequently, for reasons which we shall examine later.

1. — TAKE YOUR PALETTE, BRUSHES AND THE RAG: ARRANGE YOUR PAINTS, PREPARE AND LAY OUT THE SUPPORT...

Arrange the colours on the palette in this order from left to right: blue, madder lake, yellow, white.

Lay the Canson paper on a piece of cardboard or wooden board which is set up in an upright position resting on a chair or on the easel. Hold the brush in the usual way and...

THESE ARE THE COLOURS AND THIS IS THE ORDER YOU MUST FOLLOW

1. — Lemon Yellow Simply use white and yellow.
With the no. 8 brush, place some white in the centre of the palette and make a paste adding hardly any white spirit. Then take a little yellow and mix it with the white until you obtain a uniform colour. Do not add too much yellow at the start; it is always easier to strengthen a colour than to weaken it, adding more yellow in order to intensify the

mixture (very little yellow is needed for this) rather than adding more white to weaken it. Here and in every other mixture, you have to produce a paste-like, covering colour.

2. — Medium cadmium yellow
Just the yellow as it comes from the tube. But wait a moment: you must clean your brush since this yellow has to be placed in the centre of the palette without any trace of white, so that the paste produced is pure yellow, otherwise you will not obtain a pure strong cadmium yellow.

3. — Light orange ... ...
Yellow and a very small amount of madder lake. Notice incidentally how strong and potent madder lake is: just a touch of it can tinge and change the yellow. Do not forget then that madder lake —and Prussian blue— is capable of tinting the whole mixture when mixed with light colours.

4. — Dark orange ... ...
The same as above but with slightly more madder lake which can be added without cleaning the brush.

5. — Vermilion ... ...
Just add a little more madder lake to the dark orange. Notice, however, that we cannot produce a pure luminous vermilion... which goes to show that when we are painting under normal circumstances, it is perfectly justifiable to use other colours in addition to the three primaries.

6. — Carmine ... ...
Add madder lake to the vermilion.

7. — Dark carmine ... ...
Madder lake straight from the tube without any yellow.

8. — Very dark carmine ..
Madder lake and a very little blue.

9. — Light flesh-tint ... A lot of white, a little yellow and rather less madder lake. This is the typical flesh-tint used in very light areas to represent very luminous —and usually small— areas. When mixing this colour, remember that we have just painted a very dark carmine and so you must clean your brush thoroughly with white spirit and with soap and water in order to have an absolutely clean brush when you start on this colour.

(See No. 9 on page 76 for a sample of this colour.)

CLEAN BRUSHES, CLEAN PALETTE, CLEAN COLOURS

The exercise so far has brought out some points which are really important for successful oil-painting.

First of all: clean brushes, clean palette, clean colours. This is directly connected with what I call «the pitfall of the greys», meaning the fact that (especially when painting in oils), an inexperienced amateur finds that his colours, his pictures or, to use the professional term, his «palette» become grey and lose their purity and character.

In another of my books, «Painting», I explain that most of the problems caused by the «pitfall of the greys» are occasioned by the use and abuse of black and white as the colours which are instinctively used for darkening and lightening. We said then that in order to darken or lighten a colour —a yellow, red or blue— we must remember the range of the spectrum, that is to say the regular order of colours as shown in the rainbow (please re-read pages 52 ff. of that book, which explain this).

We can now add that, at the right time, perfect cleanliness of the paints, palette and specially the brushes also has a considerable influence when you are trying to obtain a specific colour: when his materials are not clean, the painter is liable to produce a monotonous, uncontrasted range of colours with a marked greyish tinge. Suppose, for instance, that you are painting a human face or body and require the light flesh-tint (No. 9), which is particularly suitable for highlights. Remember that no blue is used when mixing this colour and that in order to paint the face or body, you have been working with darker flesh-tints (ochres, reddish or siennas, etc.) which all contain some blue as well as yellow and red or madder lake. All your brushes are saturated with this range of flesh-tints containing blue. If you then want to produce the luminous hue of this light flesh, you must thoroughly clean one of your brushes, take clean white, clean yellow and clean red or madder lake, find a clean spot on your palette, in fact take every precaution to prevent the colours on the brushes (which contain blue) and the mixtures on the palette (which also contain blue) from spoiling the brilliance of the light flesh tint or, in other words, from making it grey and reducing the contrast.

Now bear in mind that *this rule must be obeyed in the case of every colour* in order to obtain accurate colours with a distinct personality uninfluenced by the previous mixtures. Remember that if you do not, the colours will not vibrate or stand out and each time will become dirtier and closer to that white mealy grey which is the sign of the bad amateur.

WHEN MIXING A COLOUR IN YOUR PALETTE, STRENGTHEN THE TONE BY PROGRESSIVE STAGES

This is another point which deserves a short special section.

So as not to waste paint in these early exercises, use only a little paint and try to underplay the tone. For example, if you have to mix a rosy flesh-tint, start by pasting the white and very cautiously add the madder lake and yellow, darkening the mixture by progressive stages, testing it and strengthening it in turn...

Speaking of testing, remember that when a colour is placed and mixed in the palette and seems to be the identical shade to that in the model, it may turn out to be wrong when added to the picture. The surrounding shades influence the colour. For instance, suppose you have to paint a red flower such as a carnation which in the model is placed on a white cover beside a vase, as if it had fallen out of it. Incidentally, we can be sure that this red will not be the solid red as it comes from the tube: it will need a little yellow, white, madder lake, etc. in order to produce the real colour of the model. Now imagine you are mixing this colour on the palette which, as a background, shows a sienna or dirty mahogany. *to the slight contrast offered by this dark background,* you may well produce a red which is much darker than you need (Law of successive contrasts). This is a very common occurrence and *the solution is to test the colour by means of a brush-stroke on the appropriate spot in the actual picture* in order to discover whether the colour in the palette has to be lightened or darkened.

We shall now continue with the samples of colours in the warm range:

10. — **Luminous flesh-tint** Slightly darker than before (No. 9): produced by white, with rather more yellow and madder lake but no blue.

11. — **Rosy flesh-tint** ... ...Same as before with more madder lake than yellow but still no blue. A very common colour for painting cheeks, ears, hands, etc.

12. — **Light ochre** ... ...An ochre very close to a flesh-tint: mixed from white, madder lake and yellow in very small amounts and a touch of blue.

13. — **Reddish ochre** ... ...Also one of the flesh-tints. The same as the former colour but with a little more madder lake.

14. — **Light sienna** ... ...White, yellow, madder lake and blue in that order, with more madder lake and blue than in No. 13.

15. — **Venetian red** ... ...As before but with more madder lake and less white. Before mixing this colour it would be best to clean your brush so that the clarity is not affected by the grey tint of the previous colour.

16. — **Raw umber** ... ...The same as before with rather more blue and yellow.

17. — **Light yellow ochre** Clean the brush thoroughly. Start by mixing a light lemon yellow from white and yellow. Then

13   14   15   16

21   22   23   24

produce a light green by adding a touch of blue and finally add a touch of madder lake.

18. — Yellow ochre ... ...As before but increase the amounts of yellow, madder lake and blue in the right proportions.

19. — Dark ochre ... ...Use the method described in 17 and 18. Add more yellow, blue and madder lake to No. 18 and there you are. Notice that white is not added here nor in No. 18. Remember that white «greys» a colour. At all events, there is an increased proportion of yellow.

20. — Burnt sienna ... ...Add a little madder lake to the previous colour and that's it.

21. — Grey flesh-tint ... ...White and a touch of madder lake, giving a light rose. Then a little yellow and a little blue. This is very common for painting flesh. Needless to say, you must first wash the brush thoroughly and mix the colour in a clean part of the palette, etc.

22. — Greyish rose ... ...Same as before with a little more madder lake.

23. — Light violet ... ...Add more madder lake to the previous colour.

24. — Medium violet ... ...Still more madder lake to the previous colour but no white.

25. — **Light green** ... ...Firstly, white and yellow to produce a light lemon yellow. Then a little blue to turn it green.
Finally a touch of madder lake.
You must thoroughly wash your brush and palette, «beginning afresh», in order to obtain clean colours.

26. — **Light khaki** ... ...Add yellow to the previous colour, giving a warmer tint.

27. — **Light terra verde** ...A kind of greenish khaki... or a warm green with a reddish tint, which you will obtain by adding yellow, blue and madder lake to the above (but no white).

28. —**Medium terra verde.** As before but with more yellow, blue and madder lake.

29. — **Violet light blue** ...This is a blue with a carmine tinge, a warm blue.
It is mixed from white and a little blue with just a touch of madder lake. There must be no yellow, of course. The brush must be thoroughly clean in order to produce this and the following colours.

30, 31, 32. — **Blues with a reddish tint** ... ...These blues are in the same range as No. 29 but with increasing strength. You have to add increasing amounts —in the right proportion— of blue and madder lake, without any yellow.

29   30   31   32

37   38   39   40

33 - 39. — Range of warm greys ... ... i.e. Greys with a reddish tint or rather an ochre/sienna tint. It is not necessary to clean the brush and palette. You can even try to mix these greys from the odd colours left on your palette, since if all these are mixed together, they will probably produce grey. You may, however, first obtain a bluish neutral grey... you must then clean your brush with the rag, take some white and obtain a light grey by mixing in a little of the colours left on the palette, adding yellow, madder lake and blue.

Then, to produce the following greys, you need simply add increasing amounts of each colour.

Remember that the white must be gradually overcome, making the greys darker as in No. 39, for example.

40. — Warm black ... ... Clean the brush thoroughly; mix this colour in a clean part of the palette. This and any other black must not have the least hint of white.

First mix some blue and a rather smaller amount of madder lake and even less yellow. You will then obtain a neutral black; you need simply add as much yellow and madder lake as you wish, producing a slightly reddish tint and a warm black.

41   42   43   44

49   50   51   52

RANGE OF COLD COLOURS PRODUCED FROM THE THREE PRIMARIES AND WHITE

41 - 44. — Cold yellows and flesh-tints ... ... Using a clean brush, paste some white, and add a little yellow, and minute amounts of blue and madder lake. Little yellow should be used or else the colour will acquire warmth. The same applies to the madder lake. This produces the range of cold flesh-tints which are very common in paintings of human faces and figures with a bluish tint.

45 and 46. — Cold ochres The same mixture as above but with less white and more yellow, blue and madder lake in the right proportions.

47. — Warm grey ... ... Without cleaning the brush, add a little more blue to the previous colour (and perhaps some yellow and madder lake).

48. — Dark neutral grey ... A neutral grey with a very slight coldness: it is produced from No. 47 with a very little more blue.

49. — Light green ... ... A lot of white, then yellow and blue.

50. — Bluish light green ... As before but with more blue. Notice the mealy «pastel» colour caused by the large amount of white.

45   46   47   48

53   54   55   56

Compare it with the next colour where the green is cleaner and stronger as a result of the smaller amount of white and more yellow.

51. — Light neutral green   Clean the brush to remove some of the white left over from the previous colour. Then mix blue and yellow and lighten it with white and yellow, showing the possibility of lightening a colour with yellow instead of white.

52. — Medium neutral green ... ...   Same as before, with more white, yellow and blue in the right proportions.

53. — Strong green ... ...   Merely note that there is more yellow than in the previous colour.

54. — Dark strong green   Strengthen the previous colour with blue and a little yellow.

55. — Viridian ... ...   Clean the brush to remove any traces of white and mix a little yellow with sufficient blue. Much more blue than yellow.

56. — Greenish black ... ...   A clean brush. A lot of blue, a little yellow and a touch of madder lake.

79

57	58	59	60
65	66	67	68
73	74	75	76

57. — Very light Prussian blue ... ...A lot of white and a touch of blue. Nothing else. The brush must be cleaned thoroughly with white spirit and soap and water. You must also work with a clean white and a pure blue, using a clean part of the palette.

58. — Light blue ... ...As before, with a little more blue.

59. — Sky blue ... ...As before, with more blue.

60. — Light cobalt blue ...White, blue and a touch of madder lake.

61. — Medium cobalt blue White, blue, yellow and madder lake — an extremely small amount of the last two.

62. — Medium Prussian blue ... ...Clean the brush. Mix white and Prussian blue and nothing else.

63. — Greyish blue The same Prussian blue as before with a little madder lake and a touch of yellow.

64. — Blue-black ... ...This is almost Prussian blue as it comes out of the tube: you need add just a little, a very little,

madder lake. As always when producing a black, the brush must be clean from any earlier mixtures.

65. — Light rose ... ... Clean the brush thoroughly. Mix pure white and a touch of madder lake.

66. — Carmine-rose ... ... As before with a little more madder lake.

67 & 68. — Violets ... ... White, madder lake and a touch of blue.

69 - 72. — Purple-blues ... Clean the brush and mix these purplish blues from just white, blue and a touch of madder lake, gradually increasing the amounts of the last two in order to strengthen the tone.

73 - 79. — Cold greys ... ... You already know how to obtain a grey; first mixing the colours left on the palette, then adding white and the colour or colours required to produce, in this case, a range of greys with a bluish tinge. Or you can mix grey from the three colours which is also easy enough (too easy, unfortunately!).

80. — Blue-black ... ... This is virtually the same as No. 64. Again, first wash the brush.

A SPECIFIC EXERCISE STILL USING THE THREE COLOURS

We are now going to apply the instructions given in the previous exercise to a specific subject and put your knowledge of mixing, pasting and cleaning into practice.

I would suggest that at first you paint only one simple object which entails no problems of drawing or composition, and do no more than experiment with the colour factor and the technique of oil-painting. Try this exercise with an apple, a peach, a pear or any spherical fruit which involves no problems of form but offers the widest possible range of colours.

FIRST ADVANCED STAGE (A)

Primary colours and white, clean brushes, clean palette, white spirit, rags and Canson paper.

(This is a really advanced stage as you can see from Figure A opposite: to obtain this result work as follows:)

I. — Using a flat no. 8 brush, mix a very dark grey with a reddish tinge and dilute with white spirit. Very lightly paint the circumference or shape of the apple and the shadow it casts upon the table and, with a horizontal line, lightly indicate the edge of the table against the background. Using the same colour but slightly darker, paint a few contrasting patches around the apple as you did when painting the cube (our earlier picture using burnt umber).

II. — Quickly paint the two background colours: the dark khaki of the wall and the dark sienna of the table. These are similar to the samples Nos. 28 and 16 or 20 on pp. 76 and 78.

III. — Thoroughly clean your brushes and start on the apple by applying a brilliant yellow with a slight greenish tint (white, yellow and a little blue — not much, so that the yellow remains dominant): let this spread into the shadowed areas but do not allow it to reach the right-hand edge of the fruit and also apply it to the reddish area which now has that orange shade.

IV. — A bluish grey for the edge of the shadow (clean brush), mixing it with the previous yellow which is still wet and a reddish carmine worked upwards from the lower left-hand edge until it mixes with the yellow to produce that orange-red. By mixing the orange with the bluish grey

A

— still using the same brush along the base of the apple — you will obtain that orange-grey which completes the basic shape and colouring of the fruit. A final touch of the bluish grey on the top produces the hollow of the stem... clean the brushes with the rag and... ·

SECOND AND LAST STAGE (B)

Same materials (See Figure B)

I. — Re-paint the table and background, trying to adjust the shades with a thicker layer of paint than before : you will be able to go back again to give the final touches to these tones and colours.

II. — But wait a moment... a background is not merely a splash of even colour. In the model it shows slight variations of shade. So you must try to capture these slight differences in order to give your picture a richer colouring. On the left of the khaki background, for instance, you can add a little yellow and on the right a little more blue. The more distant area of the table has more blue in it than the foreground, which becomes lighter on the right and particularly behind the apple, emphasizing the shape and volume of the fruit.

III. — Remember too that the two colours of the background and table must blend where they meet and not show a clear-cut edge: the two colours spread into each other's respective areas, (for example, behind and above the apple where a brush-stroke of the khaki background enters the dark sienna of the table).

IV. — Go back to the apple. Begin with that luminous lemonish yellow, painting not only the actual yellow area but also the orange, green and grey parts of the area in shadow. Use thicker paint where the yellow stands alone and less paint in the latter areas which must, at the end, be a reddish orange, bluish green, etc.

V. — Thoroughly clean your brushes (keeping one no. 8 for the yellow) and mix a strong red from madder lake and yellow — no white now. Now start to paint the red areas working upwards with vertical strokes which follow and model the shape (look at the example opposite).

VI. — When you reach the yellow areas, where almost accidentally you will produce an orange colour, paint with downward strokes, outlining the solid patches of orange (those near the white highlight).

VII. — By mixing blue with this orange, you will obtain the carmine-sienna tones which give the form of the apple in the shadowed areas at its base.

VIII. — A rather dirty green — with a slight amount of madder lake — will do for painting the shadow. While the paint is still wet, you can then lighten this colour and add the reflected light contained in this shadow.

IX. — Try to mix a black with a carmine tinge for painting the thin shadow along the base of the apple, turning the black into blue as you move away from the fruit into the cast shadow.

X. — When you want to blend colours, remember how you can thoroughly clean your no. 8 brush and rub the newly-painted areas with it.

XI. — Finally, make every effort to synthesize, «expressing yourself» with as few brush-strokes as possible, working out their extent, form and aim in order to obtain a spontaneous easy picture without «over-working» it by mixing and re-mixing, painting and re-painting to give a hesitant heavy and dirty finish.

XII. — Leave the highlight until last. Thoroughly clean the brush in order to produce this white light with a slight yellow tint. Apply it simply by «laying on» the painting on top of the previous coats without rubbing it.

XIII. — Easy, wasn't it? Of course, you do not need much time to paint a fruit such as this. One hour at the most during which you paint almost non-stop trying to apply the tones and colours directly without having to change them later: this is what is known as the «direct» style which we shall discuss later in this book.

To complete this first stage, I would now ask you to paint a still-life from nature using oils and only the three primaries (Prussian blue, madder lake and cadmium yellow together with white) to produce every colour. This is a kind of challenge, since I want to find out how capable you are of seeing and mixing colours, drawing and painting at the same time and generally applying the instructions given in the previous exercises.

Only one piece of advice concerning the subject: choose a simple theme containing only a few items which should also be simple in form and remember that here we are more concerned with learning how to see and interpret a colour on the basis of the three primaries, than with painting a picture.

To serve as an example, I have painted a subject similar to that suggested above and with no other purpose than to experiment with the three primary colours: I have composed the subject as simply as possible: a bottle (which we can take to contain cognac), a coffee-pot and a china cup and saucer on a dark background. There is no label on the bottle, no brandy glass, no teaspoon, no sugar-basin... just these three items.

Your still life need not, of course, be composed of these three items. You can use other objects such as earthenware pots or cooking utensils, cutlery and table-ware, food, fruits, etc. which provide a range of colour according to your taste.

SPECIFIC EXAMPLE OF A STILL-LIFE
PAINTED WITH ONLY THREE COLOURS AND WHITE

In the next page or two I shall give as a specific example the various phases of a still-life which I have painted to illustrate this exercise.

It was painted on Canson paper on a slightly larger scale than shown here, using the normal hog brushes as well as a no. 2 sable brush.

I shall now give a short description of the process:

4. — COMPOSITION or preliminary drawing: this was done with a no. 4 flat brush and left-over paint diluted with white spirit. I drew it very quickly as a sketch in order to place the items and show merely their basic form.

5. — THE FIRST STAGE (A) was painted in less than fifteen minutes: it was a matter of filling in the spacing rapidly with rather thin paint while still trying to capture the colouring and general tones of the subject.

6. — THE SECOND STAGE (B) pays more attention to the colours, especially the background and bottle, trying to fix the final general values of the subject. It already shows an awareness of the harmonization based upon greys and blues, as well as a firm idea of the composition, leaving the bottle in shadow and bringing out the tonal values of the coffee-pot and cup and saucer.

7. — THE THIRD AND LAST STAGE (C) merely shows the work put in to build up and give the objects their final form, working on the basis of the previous colouring and harmonization. Notice the following important details in this stage:

I. — The general vagueness of outlines in the more distant and shadowed areas: in the shape of the bottle whose central section blends strongly with the background, or in the shadowed outline of the coffee pot which is completely merged. On the other hand, notice that this atmospheric feeling of vagueness is not found in the shadowed edge of the cup which is thus brought more into the foreground.

II. — The colour of the highlights on the bottle appears to be white but is in fact a light grey with a greenish blue tinge. Notice too the imprecision of form, colour and volume in the cork. Both these extreme points, the highlights and the cork, were weakened intentionally to prevent them stealing attention from the coffee-pot and cup and saucer.

III. — The coffee-pot, cup and saucer are made of white china. When they were placed on the table, I could see the illuminated area as a dazzling white, vivid and brilliant. However, I did not make the mistake of painting these brilliant areas with pure white because I would not have known what white to use later to show the real highlights, those small flashes of light on the edge of the cup, saucer and the lid of the pot.

V. — Notice that the shadows contain blue... but a range of blues, containing reflections and mixtures of yellow, green, red...

AN UNEXPECTED EXERCISE

When I was finishing off this study of the coffee-pot and cup in those moments when you spend more time looking than painting, my wife came in and stood behind me looking at my work.
«Well?»... I said, anxious to know what she thought.
«Mmmmm, yes...»
She was not particularly struck. She said that the subject was poor and needed more objects... a table-cloth, a teaspoon, etc. I explained

B

that it was an exercise in oil-painting, that the subject was not meant to be elaborate and that it was just an experiment in painting with only three colours.

«Ah, I see. All the same,» she added confidently, «it's obvious that you were unable to paint with all the colours.»

She picked up a dirty rag and left.

That remark went home and worried me. «Obviously, the pupils do not need any more proof that you can paint everything with just the three primaries. All the same...»

Enough blue, madder lake and yellow were left in the palette. I added some white.

I took the studio mirror and placed it in front of me. Then I also took a sheet of watercolour paper — thick paper with a heavy grain — and immediately, without even a preliminary sketch and using a tint resembling shadowed flesh, I began to paint my self-portrait as reflected in the mirror.

Please study the colours in this rapid picture and try to find them in the sample card of 8 colours which you have already painted. Can you see? Almost every colour in this study is there in your exercise. Some of the shades are not exactly identical but you will realise that you could obtain them by adding or reducing the blue, madder lake or yellow.

There is no reason why you should not try this yourself. You may not have enough experience but that is gained by practice, by painting. You only need some more instructions on technique: details such as how to compose a background with a carbon pencil or with a basic colour before you begin to paint; or how to paint with your fingers on occasion in order to blend colours, etc. Apart from that, there is no other obstacle to prevent you from carrying out the best lesson of all — practice. So why not get out your materials and paint?

«Maria!»

It was an hour and twenty minutes later. My wife came in again and stood behind me as before.

«Using only three colours» I pointed out before she could say a word.

She looked at the palette and then at the newly painted portrait.

«It doesn't seem possible.»

There was a long silence which I imagined was caused by admiration.

«Yes, pretty good,» she said, «but...

«What's the matter now?»

«The point of your chin should be higher and your hair greyer.»

She moved away but before going out, she turned, looked at me and with a smile added the final blow.

«You should look older»... and closed the door.

HOW TO PAINT IN OILS

. . . .

You have finished practising and are now going to paint a real picture in oils with no restrictions other than those imposed by the medium itself.

This exercise will consist of a finished painting on canvas, using every colour — that is, those colours commonly employed by professional artists — in order to broaden your practical and theoretical knowledge and examine all the possibilities of expression, technique and skill. It will be an oil-painting in the full sense of the word, whose execution, being carried to the ultimate extent, will demonstrate the implications of the title «How to paint in oils».

. . . .

This is how it is to be done.

THE SUBJECT: CHOICE AND COMPOSITION

Artistic creation is not a spontaneous function. It is wrong and naïve to imagine, as a layman is apt to do, that the artist is a privileged person, driven by inspiration and expending hardly any of his own powers: inspiration does certainly not fall from the sky like manna. You have to encourage it by deliberation, sketches and hard work, in short by an intellectual process which includes observation, imagination, knowledge and experience.

A subject is usually suggested by something we have seen: a combination of forms and colours, a special effect of light and shade, of contrast and colour. This first vision may well come when we least expect it — at a bend in the road, when entering a room or looking at a child — but it cannot be. fully seen and appreciated unless you have a conscious desire to observe, see and discover.

Thus, the first requirement for finding and choosing a subject or for inspiration is cultivation of our powers of observation in order to *view* the world around us. Today or tomorrow when you go out of doors, stop looking at things subjectively, forget yourself, your worries and problems; look instead at the people, the doors and windows of the houses, the perspective of the streets and fields, the effects of light and shade on a sunny or cloudy day.

A subject for a picture and the method of painting it can also originate from something which the artist has previously imagined. In a figure study, for instance, or a still-life entitled «Small game», a mural on «Labour», etc. the objects, composition, colours, contrast, style and so on can be imagined and even sketched out without having a model in front of you. Nevertheless, when creating a preconceived subject such as this, the artist will make use of visual memories, images, forms and colours which he has seen, in fact, of his spirit of observation which is continually contributing and linking new ideas.

Indeed, the subject ceases to be a vague concept and becomes reality when the artist employs his knowledge and experience. For instance, if he is planning the «Small game» still-life, his knowledge and experience will enable him to visualize the elements of the picture, the light, the dominant colour and the general composition of the work.

Needless to say, these qualities — observation, imagination and experience — cannot be acquired overnight, but are produced by years of work, of successes and failures. So what can an amateur with no or virtually no experience do when it comes to choosing and composing a subject? Simply examine what the great artists of the past have done, study and observe, starting with the pictures in museums or in art-books, and assimilate, adapt and even «copy» shamelessly, since you must remember that this has always been the way and these same great artists did the same when they were students. Originality, creative powers and artistic temperament will come in their own good time when after some time spent in «copying» and adapting ideas, colours, and composition, you feel a natural need to change, discover and formulate one or more alterations which, as the number of your pictures increases, will lead you to find yourself and to be yourself with your own personal style.

In the meantime...

A PRACTICAL LESSON ON CHOOSING AND
COMPOSING THE SUBJECT OF A PICTURE

...In the meantime, and yet at the same time, we must continue with our studies.

. . . .

Here in my studio I am going to paint a picture and you will observe my method so that you can begin to study composition. This will be a still-life — yes, another still-life. This is not because I am addicted to still-life — I am especially keen on landscapes — but you will appreciate that a still-life is the most suitable subject for beginners. It enables one to start from scratch, choosing, arranging and composing the subject, with complete freedom to explore the possibilities and particularly to study the colours, technique and handling at one's leisure.

So let us go on... Look at this rose. I bought it this morning when thinking about the picture. And look: a death-mask of Beethoven which will also be useful.

I have been wanting to paint this subject for some time now: a vase of water with a rose, a sheet of music and Beethoven's death-mask. It came to me in a flash one day at home when my small daughter was practising «For Elise» by Beethoven, that simple piece which every beginner attempts. On top of the piano were three or four roses in a jar. I visualised the death-mask on the wall behind the roses... I thought of it as «Homage to Beethoven» or some such title... and...

You can see how yesterday afternoon I tried to formulate the subject. Just a couple of rough pencil sketches. In the first I tried to remember

and capture the image I saw that day over the piano from where I was sitting, with the light entering through half-closed shutters... but it was not right. Although I had always visualized the picture like that, when I came to transform it into a concrete sketch yesterday, I found that the viewpoint and light were unsuitable.

I then visualized a front view with the light entering from the front and side and drew the other sketch.

It seems better, doesn't it? I think the viewpoint is right with Beethoven's head at eye-level and the rose just below and in front of it. But the direction of the light... Yesterday when I finished this sketch, I felt that it could be improved with more lateral lighting, in fact a completely lateral light so that Beethoven's face is half in shadow and half in light.

Let's try this. We shall then see how it comes out in practice.

We place a rather low table against the wall — I intend to paint seated — and above it, on the wall, we hang the death-mask; on the table beneath it we put a vase of water containing a rose; and behind the vase the rolled-up sheet of music «For Elise». Do you see? Let me find out which is the best position for the rose... that's it. Come over here. Sit down. This will be more or less where I shall sit when painting: about 8 feet from the subject. Make a note of this:

**Distance from the subject:
approximately eight feet.**

But, of course, this cannot be taken as a general rule as you will see.

HOW FAR FROM THE SUBJECT?

Well... there is no fixed distance. It always depends upon the size of the subject: the smaller it is, the closer you should be and vice versa. You should be able to see the entire subject with one glance all the time you are working. If this subject included the piano with someone playing it, we should have to place ourselves much further back — at least 5 to 6 yards. Thus we can formulate the rule:

Generally speaking, the distance between the artist and the subject depends upon the size of the latter and, as far as possible, the ability to view it as a whole. Therefore, the distance is greater for a large subject than for a small one.

FIRST ATTEMPT IN COMPOSING THE SUBJECT (A)

(In this and the following attempts, please follow the photographs A, B, C, etc.)

How's that? Not bad, is it? But the first point that comes to mind is that the mask is smaller here than in the sketch I drew yesterday. I did in fact visualize it as being larger in relation to the rose. But we can solve this problem later by reducing or enlarging the size while painting. At this point, we shall just consider the arrangement and composition of the objects.

What about the light? It falls very well on the rose and the head, as you can see: I was right to «split» the mask. This gives more emphasis and, incidentally, the whole form is simpler, less conspicuous and more firmly fixed in the middle distance so that the rose stands out in the foreground. This leads us to one of the basic rules of composition:

Every picture must contain a strong centre of interest or principal feature which stands out in relation to all the other objects.

We must ask ourselves what we are intending to paint in this picture: which of these items — the head or the rose — best expresses and synthesizes the idea of «homage». I settle for the rose. So the rose is to be the centre of interest in this picture. Beethoven's mask will also be included but in the middle distance as something imprecise with little contrast.

In view of this I feel that this first attempt is not satisfactory: it provides too much variety to the detriment of unity. As you know, the first and most important rule of composition tells us to seek for:

Variety within the context of unity

This rule is not obeyed in this present composition. Look at it (Figure A): the head is too distant from the vase and rose, requiring a large picture which reduces the importance of the elements and scatters them. The mask is isolated, forming a centre of interest in itself, distracting and reducing the attention which should be focused on the rose.

THIS IS A VERY COMMON MISTAKE
BY INEXPERIENCED AMATEURS

In my years as a teacher I have corrected hundreds of drawings and paintings whose main fault was to reduce and isolate the various objects in the model. There were pictures whose elements seemed to be scattered without any connection between them, so that each formed a centre of interest and attention which completely destroyed the unity of the work. You must not make this elementary mistake! Remember that the subject must be arranged and framed in such a way that the objects occupy a large part of the picture while, at the same time, they must not be lost against a wide background. Remember too how some forms can be placed in front of others, forming a series of planes which promote the general unity.

SECOND ATTEMPT (B)

It is obvious what must be done: the mask must be lowered closer to the rose.

There it is (B). A perfect solution and now we can begin to paint...

But wait a moment. We must not be satisfied with just this: we must try every possibility. A good professional does not accept the first idea even if it is satisfactory. What if we study the possibility of making the subject richer by adding some more objects?

THIRD ATTEMPT (C)

For instance, book... books, music, Beethoven... they are all linked. Let's see (Figure C).

No. You can see what happens: the shape and tone of the books when placed on the left disrupt and destroy the main feature: the rose, its leaves and the arabesque which they form or rather did form when set against the bare wall.

Let's try the other side:

FOURTH ATTEMPT (D)

That's better. Especially since the shadow of the books on the wall forms a dark background against which the rose is more prominent. But...

Those books! The shape of the book... the upright backs and the light colour of the first one, the thickest... it won't do. By adding the books we have simply called attention to other shapes to the detriment of the centre of interest, the rose.

I'll tell you what to do. Why not try to increase the impact of the centre of interest, perhaps by making it more important and using a jar instead of a glass vase? ...by adding another flower?

FIFTH ATTEMPT (E)

Certainly a radical change but I think we are on the right lines. The bud and the rose now dominate the scene and play a larger part than before. The small copper jar provides a pleasant note of colour and draws attention by its tone, form and colour, helping to emphasise the flowers as the foreground.

I have had to raise the mask in an attempt to form an L-shape with the model closer to the edge, forming the stroke of the L on the left, and with the sheet of music and the table as the horizontal stroke.

But this L-shape is not successful since it overloads the left-hand side.

SIXTH ATTEMPT (F)

I have moved the table to the left and placed the rose in the centre. In the last analysis, the rose is the «star» of the picture. I think that when it comes down to it, *the centre is its correct position*. I have also moved the sheet of music and — notice this detail — have placed the largest and lightest book behind the stem of the bud so that it becomes more prominent since the dark shape of the leaves and the stem stand out against the light colour of the book (compare the difference between Figures E and F).

SEVENTH ATTEMPT (G)

It is possible to improve it even further by lowering the mask and so reducing the size of the picture and enlarging the objects in it, which gives more unity.

EIGHTH ATTEMPT (H)

Excuse me for changing my mind again but I have found a new arrangement. I just removed the books for a moment in order to see whether they were in the way and, as you can see, realised that without them the leaves and stem of the bud become even more prominent and are brought more into the foreground. And so...

NINTH ATTEMPT (I)

Take the books away. Let's go back to the beginning but with a better idea of what we want. Do you see? With the flowers in the centre of the picture and the mask behind... but wait: the leaves «tickle Beethoven's nose». That must be remedied.

TENTH ATTEMPT (J)

I raise the mask and move the branch to the left but... the subject is becoming scattered, the space on the right is unsatisfactory and, moreover, the leaves are now touching the chin.

I don't want to lose the contrast between the bud and the background caused by the bud being placed exactly in front of the shadow cast by the mask, which emphasises the shape of the bud and gives it prominence owing to the illuminated shape being set against a shadowed background.

One thing has been improved all the same: the position of the leaves which now form an arabesque which I intend to retain.

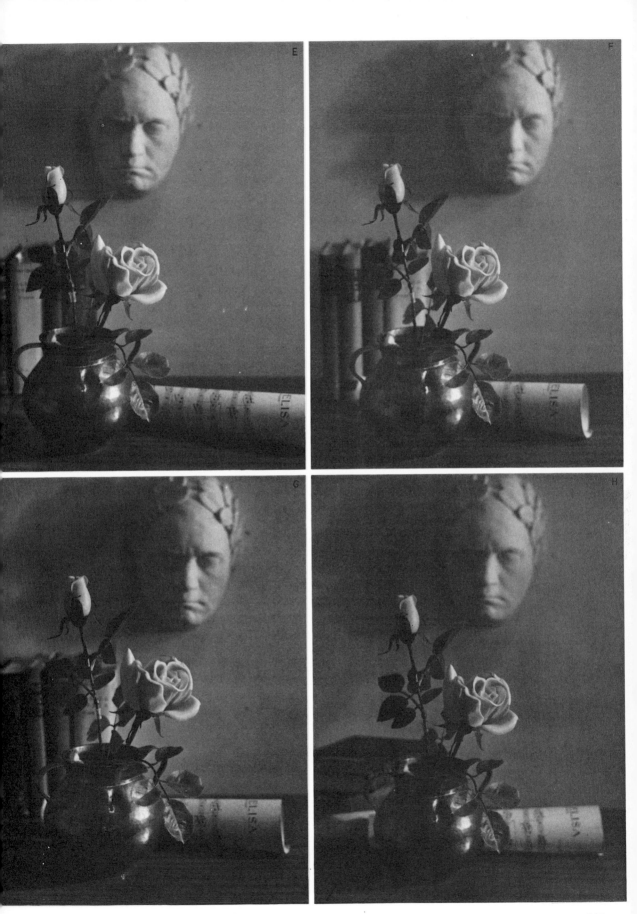

ELEVENTH ATTEMPT (K)

Bring the mask down behind the rose: the sheet of music more to the right in order to justify the space there and...

FINAL COMPOSITION (L)

At last. This is the best framework, the most successful way of inter-relating the objects or, in other words, the best composition.

As you have seen, a composition cannot be decided upon in a matter of minutes but has to be studied thoroughly, so that every possibility is tried in order to produce the best result: testing and re-testing time and again. This is the maxim of this lesson which I hope you will bear in mind in your future work.

INTERPRETATION

The artist is now sitting (or standing) in front of the model with the easel and canvas before him. The palette, paints and brushes are waiting beside him within easy reach.

He takes a black crayon, raises his arm, looks at the model... it seems as if he is going to draw but no: without taking his eyes from the model, he lowers his hand, puts down the pencil, sits back in his chair and, still looking at the model, lights a cigarette. Five minutes... ten minutes... his gaze is still fixed attentively on the model, following its forms, comparing spaces, colours, volumes...

Then, more relaxed, he begins to draw with a sure hand.

That is more or less what happens. In those minutes before he begins to paint, this is what the artist does: *pauses to study the model*, looks at it critically, examines the best way of interpreting it, decides what he is going to do and how he is going to do it. You must do this yourself when you paint: pause to study, calculate and decide.

Let's say that I am going to paint and have stopped to study and work out what I am going to do. Imagine that I am thinking aloud:

«The jar is big. Too much jar for so few flowers: I'll paint it smaller. The head, the rose... head... rose... yes, the head is small: I'll paint it larger. And... of course! Why not cut it short at the forehead? That's it: I can concentrate the picture more, increasing and bringing out the centre, the rose. I'll also lower the bud by shortening the stem... down to the level of the chin. What about colours? A creamish-yellow as a dominant with siennas, reds... pinks. But, I'm not so sure... let's try it anyhow. (I pick up the crayon, face the canvas)... here, in the centre, the rose. The head up to here...»

(I start to draw).

THE FIRST PHASE:
DRAWING OR CONSTRUCTING THE WORK

«Are we going to draw or paint?»

Some time ago there was a lot of argument about how to begin a painting; some claimed that it is best to draw and construct the model first (with crayon, brush and liquid paint, etc.) while others said it is better to paint directly on the clean canvas without any preliminary sketch.

In reply to this, Waetzoldt, the art professor and critic, justifiably claimed in his book «Art and You», that: «Classicism has caused artists to see colours as a kind of cover for objects which can be visualized without colour. Generations of painters have accepted this so that instead of constructing in colour, they colour a drawing and by that colour convert it into a painting. An inborn painter,» Waetzoldt claims, «does not see the shape first and then the colour but sees the colours in conjunction with the form, and the coloured forms as a natural combination: he does not «colour» his drawings like a child, but paints.»

The Renaissance chronicler, Vasari, tells us that Titian «employed colours immediately without any preliminary drawing». Titian himself said that this «was the real and best way of working and was true drawing» (meaning that he drew as he painted).

At the same period and in the same place, however, another celebrated artist: Michelangelo, slyly commented in relation to Titian's method «It is a pity that in Venice they do not begin by learning to draw properly».

To list only a few of the ancient and contemporary masters, Michelangelo, Rubens, David, Degas and Dali were or are addicted to constructing and drawing —some of them with considerable enthusiasm— before starting to paint. Velasquez, on the other hand, said that «he did not prepare his pictures and sometimes did not even draw them. He worked *alla prima*, starting on the canvas immediately with a brush». Sorolla considered that «a brush with thin oil-paint» —(such as you have been using in the previous exercises)— «is sufficient for indicating the proportions and placing of the objects on the canvas». The same author says that Sorolla often started on a work without any preliminary drawings and then began to «daub» the canvas, covering it very quickly.

I feel that no matter which technique they preferred, everyone would agree with the rule formulated by Waetzoldt:

An inborn painter does not see the shape first and then colour but sees the colours in conjunction with the form, and the coloured forms as a natural combination.

This is undoubtedly the logical answer and I think that it would be accepted by any artist, whether he draws or not, paints directly or constructs the model in advance, putting in as much detail as he wishes.

So in the case of an amateur without much experience —by «experience» I mean years of painting every Sunday and bank holiday— I am convinced that he must first draw and construct the basic picture before beginning to paint. In my years as an art teacher I have found over and over again that many pupils' paintings are worthless since the drawing is not given sufficient importance. I have also found that, despite their eager desire to learn, many amateurs are unable to control their impatience and irresistible desire to see the picture finished, which is bound to lead to failure due to their haste and lack of preliminary study.

To sum up: if you already have the gift of being able to frame, draw and work out dimensions and proportions without any trouble and with complete accuracy, then if you like, you can paint directly without any preparations... or simply draw a few lines to fix the positions, dimensions and proportions of the objects in the model. If, on the other hand, you are aware that drawing is your weak point, then you should conscientiously work on the construction, bearing in mind that it is the final result which really counts. Nobody asks *how a picture has been done:* people look at and admire *what has been done.*

On the next two pages you can see our picture: (a) constructed with a few simple crayon lines which sketch in the basic shapes of the objects within the framework of a preliminary drawing which fixes the frame, position, proportions and the dimensions of each object. From this you can begin to paint immediately. However (b) shows the same drawing elaborated almost to the final stage: a finished crayon drawing in which I have tried to give values to the model and assess the general tonal effect.

Choose your own system in keeping with your abilities.

METHODS FOR DRAWING
OR CONSTRUCTING AN OIL-PAINTING

Whatever surface you use for painting —canvas, paper, cardboard, wood— the methods and media commonly employed for drawing the model are as follows:

BRUSH-DRAWING WITH RATHER LIQUID OIL-PAINT

You already know this method since you employed it in the previous exercises. I will simply add that a drawing of this type may consist of a few strokes of the brush as a means merely for framing and placing the model, or it may be a finished drawing which even examines the light and shade effects. In either case, it is usual to work with just one colour which is relevant to the general tones of the subject or can be simply a medium grey which is the most suitable. Rubens employed this

a)

b)

method and painted the values with a dark ochre in some areas, and a lighter ochre in others, which provided him from the very beginning with an excellent tone structure over which he could paint the flesh-tints of his figures. The method is still used by some contemporary artists.

DRAWING IN RED CHALK

Red chalk with its reddish sienna colour has also been used by many artists, especially in the past. It can be very successful in figure studies and portraits. The method is to draw the lines with the chalk and then soften them with the finger. When the drawing is finished, it should be rubbed lightly with a clean rag in order to remove any surplus chalk.

DRAWING WITH BLACK CRAYON

This is the most common medium and is considered to be the classic method for drawing on canvas The rough texture of the canvas enables the smooth crayon to «take» and produce lines with astonishing ease and also makes it possible to soften the lines quickly with the finger which produces a very artistic effect. On the other hand, owing to the instability of the crayon, it is easy to use a rubber to form outlines, put in the highlights, etc. (See illustrations (a) and (b): the latter in particular shows the touches of the rubber in the rose, vase and sheet of music). As well as being unstable, the crayon does not adhere completely to the canvas and becomes minute particles of powder which only just manage to stick in the interstices of the canvas. Obviously it is not advisable to apply oils over such a drawing since this may well make the colours dirty, especially white and the light colours. So after you have studied the construction —and the values, if you like— wipe the canvas with a clean rag in order to remove the loose powder. This will almost completely wipe out the drawing and leave only a slight indication which is, however, quite enough for painting.

But why do we make a drawing and work out a construction with all the lights and shades, tones and contrasts, if only a slight indication of it is left after being wiped with the rag? I would reply that you do this to make sure, to test and to fix the forms in your mind, providing a memory which the artist can use for painting —«drawing» with colours, tones and patches of paint— with more likelihood of success.

Finally, it is not advisable to draw with a lead pencil and then paint over it in oils, since the graphite in the pencil can darken and stain the paint as it is drying. For the same reason, you definitely must not use a coloured pencil.

WHERE AND HOW TO BEGIN PAINTING WITH OILS

Most of the old masters, Titian, Veronese, Leonardo, Rubens, Velasquez and Rembrandt started their figure studies by first painting the areas in shadow, implying that they were concerned about the three-dimensional form —the drawing and relief— as well as the colour. Chardin, one of the most famous painters of the 18th Century, «first painted the dark areas, by applying a thin coat of paint». Renoir used the same method but did not make it an absolute rule: in his portraits and figures «he usually began with diluted paint and just a trace of colour, painting the dark shadows. Then he went over it thoroughly.»

After drawing a very quick sketch, Cézanne sometimes painted from the edge of the picture towards the figure whose details he left until last. Strange as this method may seem, it does essentially follow the rule of first filling in the background, that is to say, the largest area.

If we remember that the old masters almost always painted over a *coloured drawing*, i.e. a drawing «painted» with oils of one or two colours which from the start tone with the dominant colour planned for the picture (Veronese, for instance, used a greenish ochre colour), or otherwise they painted on coloured canvases (Velasquez, used canvas primed with a reddish sienna), it is easy to see why the idea of first painting the darker areas was prevalent. The method is still valid today, especially for figures and portraits.

In modern painting, however, since we usually paint on white canvas with very luminous paints, and are more concerned with colour contrasts, obviously the painter's first problem is to eliminate the white of the canvas so as to avoid mistakes in relation to his contrasts... and colours.

I will explain this: in accordance with the law of simultaneous contrasts, you will remember that when we paint a dark colour over a white background, the colour appears to be darker than when we see it surrounded by other tones and colours. For instance, we could say that when we are painting a red flower on a white background, a very bright rose colour —but not a strong red— is enough to give the impression of the real colour. If we then paint the background black, the flower will appear pale red, not bright enough, just as if we have really lowered the red of the flower.

On the other hand, if we allow for the *law of induction or «sympathy» of complementary colours*, this white background will produce a greenish tint in the red of the flower and around the flower, since green is the complementary of red.

Laws of contrast:

Simultaneous contrasts:

1. A light colour becomes paler in proportion to the darkness of its surrounding colour and similary a dark colour becomes darker in proportion to the lightness of its surrounding colour.

2. If two colours of different tones are placed side by side, this strengthens both of them, making the light one lighter and the dark one darker.

Law of maximum contrast:

Maximum contrast of colour is produced by placing two complementaries side by side.

Law of induction of complementary colours:

To change any colour, it is only necessary to change the colour of its surrounding background.

Chevreul's law:

When a brush-stroke of colour is placed on a canvas, it not only tints the canvas with the colour on the brush but also colours the surrounding area with its complementary.

All these laws give us a general rule which answers the question: «Where do I begin?»

BEGIN BY PAINTING THE LARGEST AREAS

In nearly every case these areas will be those which are least specifically defined by the construction and drawing: the background in a still-life, portrait or figure-study; the sky in a landscape; the sea in a seascape, and so on. Your still-life may contain a table, a cloth or a rather large object, or the landscape may have hills or fields, bushes or trees which take up a large area. So start with these large areas and try to fill them in as soon as possible, to paint and eliminate the flat background of the support even —and sometimes, especially— when that background is grey, ochre or red.

HOW?

How do you start to paint a picture in oils? With a lot or little relief? Pale or strong colours? How much detail?

In an attempt to answer these and other questions, I am going to give a short lesson on the most common oil-painting techniques:

THE MOST COMMON OIL-PAINTING TECHNIQUES

Leaving aside the spatula technique for the moment, we can distinguish between techniques which are commonly used by a professional artist: these are *direct painting*, where the painter works on fresh paint, and *painting in stages*, where the picture is completed in several sessions and the artist works on dry or semi-dry paint.

DIRECT PAINTING

We can expand the above definition by saying that:

**With direct painting, the picture is
completed in one or more sessions
but the paint must always be fresh,
wet or partially wet.**

As you will appreciate, the most common type of this technique are paintings which have been completed in one session. These include drafts and sketches in general, rapid sketches and notes, as well as a large proportion of modern and contemporary finished works for which the artist has only allowed himself one session in an attempt to capture a more forceful and spontaneous effect. We can mention in this connection the number of *rapid painting competitions* which are now held in many places: in these events the time allowed is a maximum of four or five hours and the painting must deal with a specific subject or locality.

Can you appreciate the conditions under which such a picture can be completed in one session of four or five hours?

**1. From the very beginning, the picture has to be
painted with a mind to the final effect.**

This is one particular way of starting on a picture: keeping the final effects in mind right from the start and so arranging the strength, contrast and harmonization of the colours from the very first brushstroke. With this technique, you cannot have second thoughts or «leave it for a moment and then we shall see», nor can you correct it by scraping off the paint with a spatula as you can with other methods, since this would destroy the light touch and spontaneity which characterize this technique.

> **2. From the very beginning, the artist has to decide immediately and simultaneously upon the construction, relief and colours without any second thoughts being possible.**

Not asking much, is it? When you paint over several sessions, you hint at the colour of an object, apply it rather evenly since you know you can come back and give it form by painting in lights and shades. Nor do you bother too much about the shapes since you can correct them at subsequent sessions. In other words, you underplay the colour with the intention of strengthening it later when the general effect has been elaborated. But the direct technique does not have these advantages: you must draw, shade, lighten, give shape and colour simultaneously, irrevocably.

> **3. From the very beginning the picture is usually painted with thick paint.**

This is conditioned by the two earlier points and also by the artist's own preference, the subject being painted, etc. Under the circumstances described, where rapid, impressionistic work is required, the artist may well decide to use thick paint.

Here is some technical advice for painting this type of picture:

— *Draw with a brush dipped in paint and white spirit, using a dark colour —grey, bluish grey or sienna, according to the dominant colour— and fill in all the dark areas.*

— *Start by painting the large areas with a very thin first coat, well-diluted with white spirit: this forms a kind of wash which immediately cancels out the white of the canvas and produces an approximate tone.*

— *Mix the correct colour and with thick or thickish paint immediately cover the largest areas which do not require detailed work.*

— *Paint the remainder, keeping the colours completely separate —clean brushes, clean palette— and bring out the volume, first by means of planes and then, immediately afterwards, by mixing and blending adjoining colours.*

— *Put in the last small details with sable brushes and paint diluted with linseed oil or a little turpentine.*

This last piece of advice enables one to draw and paint lines, small patches of colour, little touches, etc. or in other words, to paint small shapes on very wet, recently-painted areas. You cannot, of course, put in a lot of work on these touches: you should «deposit» the paint rather than apply it by actual brush-strokes.

In fact, this is really a difficult technique but it can produce superb results when the artist has full mastery of drawing, relief and colours.

DIRECT PAINTING IN SEVERAL SESSIONS

The same problems arise in the case of direct painting in several sessions but they are less extreme.

The picture is begun with one or two thin coats —one in each session— which are mixed from oil-paint and plenty of white spirit, but not enough to make the paint runny. The first or first and second sessions, as the case may be, are comparatively short. The sole intention is to give as close an approximation as possible to the final tones. The coats are thin because between the sessions —an interval of several hours— the paint can take, without being completely dry, so that the tones can be corrected.

You use the real direct technique in the last session when you draw, form and paint the final result with heavier layers of paint which can be as thick as the artist wishes.

As an example of direct painting —probably completed in two sessions— look at the section of Cézanne's «Blue Jar» overleaf which is now in the Louvre, Paris. Note the extremely thin background paint to which has been added a later, thicker coat (see this detail in the orange-coloured apple on the right and in the yellow-ochre background of the table). Look at that thin line which outlines the form of the apple, rounding it and you will realise that Cézanne painted it with a sable brush and paint diluted with linseed-oil. Notice that here and there this direct method has called for such quick and spontaneous work that small areas of the canvas remain uncovered. See too how concerned the artist was to enrich the colours, overcoming the monotony of constant colours and tones by speckling them with similar colours. Finally, notice how he encourages contrasts by emphasising outlines in order to make them stand out from their backgrounds.

TECHNIQUE OF PAINTING IN STAGES

This is the peaceful, unhurried method used by the old masters and still employed nowadays for some comparatively large portraits and figure-studies. Essentially, it is based on the idea of splitting up and organizing the work. It can be defined thus:

When painting by stages, the method is to complete the picture in several sessions, painting on dry or semi-dry paint and distinguishing between the drawing and modelling on the one hand and the colours on the other.

Right from the start, this technique is completely different from direct painting. When painting in stages, the first concern is to draw and model, putting in light and shade, and the colours are a secondary factor for the time being. When the construction has been completed after two or more sessions, the colour is given attention and is also applied in several sessions, allowing time for the paint to be dry or almost dry and then gradually adding colour in accordance with the strength and contrasts required.

The first stage —drawing and modelling— begins with thin coats of almost monochrome paint: a grey with slight touches of warm or cold colours depending upon the range decided upon in advance, or a greenish ochre, a reddish sienna, etc. The entire picture is drawn and modelled with the help of white and the values and contrasts thoroughly explored.

Thicker coats of the real colour are then applied on this solid background. The early thin coats are painted with white spirit as the solvent and no linseed oil, while the top coats comprise oil-paints as they come from the tube or diluted with more linseed oil than white spirit.

The absorptive powers of the early coats assist in drying the top coats, allowing the artist to paint and re-paint to produce dragged brush work and rubbed work.

When they came to paint the top coats —the real painting as opposed to the preliminary coats —some old masters employed the direct painting method in several sessions which produced a freer and more spontaneous style.

«THICK ON THIN»

You will have noticed that, although each technique employs different methods, direct painting and painting in stages have one feature in common, namely that *the first coat must always be thin and diluted with white spirit*.

This brings us to one last theoretical point before we finally return to our practical exercise: we must examine an ancient rule of oil-painting which still has to be followed today, namely that paint must be applied «Thick on thin».

We must begin by defining these terms:

THIN PAINT contains little or no oil. Tempera or gouache are examples of this, as is oil-paint when mixed with white spirit which dilutes and reduces the amount of oil.

THICK PAINT contains normal or large amounts of oil. Oil-paint as it comes from the tube contains a certain amount of oil which we can consider the normal amount: when it is mixed or dissolved in linseed oil, it contains a large amount of oil.

The ancient rule of «thick on thin» means that:

Good oil-painting requires a thin basic or first coat over which must be applied the subsequent coats of thick paint.

The old masters carried this to such an extreme that they painted the basic or first coat with egg-tempera (nowadays tempera or gouache could well be used instead for the same purpose) over which they then painted with oils. Most of the Renaissance artists used this method. Velasquez is supposed to have painted his celebrated portrait of Pope Innocent X in this way.

Nowadays there is no need to carry this to such an extreme and few if any contemporary artists apply oil-paints onto a thin background of gouache or tempera. As far as we are concerned, the following is sufficient:

**To obey the rule of «thick on thin»,
remember that the first coat must
be painted with more white spirit
than the subsequent coats.**

All right, you say, but why all this thick-and-thin business in the first place?

There are two important reasons: first and foremost, because if you paint «thick on thin» you can be certain that your picture will keep better and not suffer any real disasters.

We have already seen that, when oil-paints are diluted with white spirits, they lose their oil, become more liquid and thinner: they are thinned down, in fact. Remember too that white spirit dries very rapidly by evaporation and so thin paint dries rapidly and efficiently.

On the other hand, thick paint containing oil dries slowly and, what is worse, misleadingly. If you apply some oil-paint to a canvas just as it comes from the tube, within four or five days a kind of skin will probably have formed over it: this will appear to be dry but, in fact, the rest of the paint beneath it is still wet and pasty. As it dries, this paint will contract and shrink the outer layer. When the paint is really dry after two or three weeks, the squirt of paint will look like an empty wine skin. Now if this thick oily paint had been applied on a thin base, the «empty wine skin» effect would have been the only result, but imagine that four or five days after painting this thick layer, you apply a coat of thin paint over it. Can you guess what would happen? The thin coat would dry quickly, forming a hard, compact but thin crust, so thin that it would be unable to resist the shrinking and distortion of the «skin» and would eventually split, gaining the characteristic appearance of cracked paintings.

(See below a portion of Velasquez's «Woman with a fan» which crearly shows how the paint has cracked).

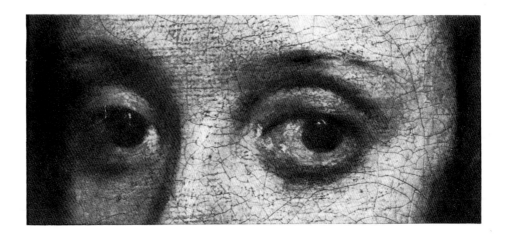

The second important reason for the «thick on thin» rule can best be explained by the fact that, if the first is thin, it dries rapidly, so that (the next day, for instance), you can paint on a dry or half-dry surface which enables you to touch up, re-paint, etc. without the previous colours having any effect upon your work.

There are a few things left which you need to know about oil-painting. The canvas with the still-life of Beethoven's head and the roses is still waiting, drawn, constructed and ready for painting. You are still here beside me in my studio waiting to see what I am going to do. So, let us study these few things while we are painting.

AND NOW TO PAINT

The palette... brushes... paints...

With all the brushes and the entire range of colours commonly used by professional artists and arranged around the palette in the usual order: white —a large amount of it— at the top right, then cadmium yellow, yellow ochre... and so on.

FIRST STAGE: General modulation of the colours

---

1. — I begin with the background, applying a thin coat (so thin that the grain of the canvas can be seen in the illustration of this first stage overleaf). For this colour I use plenty of white, mixed with yellow ochre, burnt umber, and ultramarine blue. I dilute with white spirit. I increase the amount of ultramarine blue when I reach the lower right-hand section. On the left I add more umber and a touch of red.

2. — I now paint the shadow cast by Beethoven's mask using the same colour as the background plus cobalt blue, umber and a little carmine.

3. — I go on to the mask itself: I change the previous colour by adding white and ultramarine blue. I apply a few lighter touches with a very little ochre and rather more white, painting the reflected light.

4. — I forgot to mention that I am using a hog brush, no. 12 flat.

5. — I now paint the table with the no. 8 brush: ochre, umber, red, a touch of carmine, a little viridian (green) ... perhaps I need a touch of white... I get it right by adding a little of the background colour which contains white *and is dirty.*

«DIRTY COLOURS»

Titian is said to have recommended «dirty colours», meaning that one should never paint with strident, discordant colours. Indeed Nature contains almost no absolute colour such as a pure red, or a pure yellow. We only paint with such colours to produce a specific effect. But as a rule when we want to copy nature, we must follow Titian's advice and «in most cases add blue» since blue is closest to grey and is the colour of shadows, space and atmosphere.

6. — I paint the jar: no. 8 brush again with the colour it already carries plus umber, red, carmine, emeraude green...

7. — Now to the sheet of music: with the no. 12 brush which still carries the warm grey of Beethoven's mask, I first paint the darkest strip along the centre of the rolled-up sheet. Just an ordinary strip of colour. Then I clean the brush with the rag and take up some white and yellow. I mix this together and almost automatically obtain the yellowish grey of the reflected light. I paint and blend, shading (after wiping the paint off the brush with the rag) the dark grey of the first strip into the yellowish grey of the reflected light. Finally, with a flat no. 4 brush and clean white, I paint and shade the upper illuminated section.

8. — I move on to the rose, using the two no. 4 brushes.
   Please take note of these colours:

> *Clean* white and *clean* red for the light roses.
> White, a touch of carmine and cobalt blue for the shadowed section of the petal which seems to be rolled up.
> Yellow and ochre, with red, for the orange reflections (which are lightened by means of the first rose colour in order to improve harmonization).
> Carmine, umber and red. Here and there I add a touch of Prussian blue and, where suitable, lighten it with the rose colour of the highlights in order to produce harmonized colours.

These four colours are all I need for painting the rose and the bud.

9. — Finally the leaves: for those on the upper half of the bud's stem, I use viridian (green) and burnt umber with some carmine and ultramarine blue where I think it advisable (I really mean ultramarine, which makes the mixture greyer). The dominant colour will, of course, be provided by the viridian colour. For the other leaves, I use the same colour, but lighten it with ochre and red (no white needed here!). If necessary, I can add yellow.

THE FIRST STAGE

SECOND STAGE: General adjustment of the colours

«Now, let's see whether we are on the right lines with this first stage.»

«What do you mean?» you ask.

Well, I didn't say anything before but —you may have noticed this— for a short time this morning, the sun went in, like it is now and the studio here was tinged with a blue light. Not much, but it lost something of that golden warm atmosphere which had prevailed until then. I felt that a bluish-green background would provide a better contrast than the creamy background of the first stage.

There is no question about it now. Why did I not realise it before? The flowers are rose-coloured, but the tonal colours —the shadow— have an orange, vermilion and even red tint. The complementary of red is green. A background of strong green would provide the maximum contrast with the red but it would have an unpleasant effect due to the similarity of tone. However, a light green background with a slight tinge of blue would be bound to produce perfect harmony of colour within an equally strong contrast of colour.

That is how it is, at least in theory. There is a rule about this which it is worth remembering:

Two complementaries whose tones are dissimilar, produce excellent harmonization.

In practice... well, we shall see.

10. — I repaint the background using the same colour as before but, after adding viridian, ultramarine blue and a very little burnt umber.

11. — No, that won't do. I must clean my brush with the rag and make a new mixture which contains a little yellow and ochre as well as the previous colours.

12. — That's it. It's not such a clean background colour as I wanted but it will have to do for the time being.

13. — Of course, I must re-adjust the tone of the shadow cast on the wall and the shadow of Beethoven's mask: I use the same range of colour by adding ultramarine blue and a little carmine in the shadow. On the mask I apply the new background colour with white and ultramarine blue.

14. — The table, sheet of music and jar now contain slightly more green and burnt umber (see the illustration opposite which corresponds to the second stage).

15. — I have spent over a quarter of an hour on the rose and still can't get it right. It is best to rub out what I have done and start afresh.

THE SECOND STAGE

STARTING AGAIN FROM SCRATCH

I had to do it —there was no other way! Not that the rose in the first stage was a model of perfection —far from it— but it is always annoying when you have to go back.

You must do the same yourself when you have to. Bear in mind that you will always gain by it. And see how easy it is:

I. — Make a round bundle of clean rag. Rub it gently over the painted area.

II. — Change the rag for a new piece and there you are. The advantage of this method is that a trace of the previous colour is always left, a dirty greyish trace over which it is astonishingly easy to paint.

Now that we are on the subject, I should mention that this job can also be done with a spatula, removing the paint by passing it flat along the canvas. This is especially necessary when the paint has been applied in a thick coat. After the spatula has removed the layer, the rag is used as before for cleaning off the rest of the paint.

---

16. — It was worth the trouble. The rose came right in no time at all with much more detail and colour than before. I should have mentioned that before painting it, I outlined it with a thick line of umber and Prussian blue —almost black— well diluted with white spirit. I did the same in the first stage, as you noticed.

17. — Of course, when I was painting and repainting the background, I spoilt some of the leaves by spreading the background colour over them. It doesn't matter: I paint them again and rather larger —notice this detail— and again outline their shape by spreading some of the back-ground colour onto them... until... let's leave it until tomorrow.

THIRD AND LAST STAGE: General adjustment and finishing touches

---

Good morning. These hours of rest have been put to good use. They always are, since when the picture is left for a while, the artist has time to think about, to forget it a little and, when he comes back to it the next day, he sees new aspects, shades and colours in the model. He is also more capable of noticing his own faults and correcting them. In our picture, the white spirit has overcome the impermeability of the canvas and the paint has taken enough for us to be able to complete the work in one session of direct painting.

---

18. — The paint I now use is thick enough to cover the grain of the canvas.

THIRD AND LAST STAGE

19. — Once more I start with the background. A few tests, a few uncertainties and I've got it: viridian green, yellow, ochre, umber and ultramarine blue. And white, of course. In the upper right-hand section I emphasise the yellowish tendency and, below it and on the left, I use more ultramarine blue and viridian.

20. — I go back to the mask: as before, I use the background colour with burnt umber and ultramarine blue for the shadows. In the middle of the illuminated section of the head, I apply a white which has been slightly tinted, mixed or dirtied with the background colour and a rather obvious amount of ultramarine blue. This ultramarine blue and clean white is ideal for showing the highlights (clean brush, clean palette, clean colours — remember?). I have added some Prussian blue in the shadow to make it more luminous and transparent.

21. — I am concerned about the construction of the head. Luckily, in direct painting, oils are the ideal medium for changing and correcting forms.

22. — I lighten the shadow on the sheet of music. I paint the staves, notes and signs, not precisely but, as you can see, vaguely and solely as a form of indication, although each is correctly placed and coloured (lighter in the illuminated section than in the shadowed area): a greenish grey with umber...

23. — I have gone back to the head: «painting» with the tip of the little finger, I have slightly moved the line of shadow by the nose... I have corrected the position of the wrinkle which starts at the edge of the nostril over the commissure. I paint and correct with my finger merely by taking up light paint and scraping it in order to cover and move the dark shape. It is very easy: try it.

PAINTING WITH THE FINGERS

The first mention of this trick is made by Leonardo da Vinci and Titian, but all the Renaissance painters probably used it. Indeed, Titian painted not only with all his fingers but also with the edge of his hand: I have done this myself with very good results.

Needless to say, you do not pick up paint with your fingers and apply it to the picture, as you do with a brush, but use the fingers to work over sections which have already been painted.

I must explain, however, that this technique is only used from time to time in order to obtain specific effects. It is particularly useful for fine blending or shading and also for making slight alterations to points where the light and shade meet. It is used primarily in portraits and figures studies as well as for other subjects in which the drawing, forms and colours must be very accurate. In the mask of Beethoven, for example, the fingers were used on many occasions for forming, shading and blending. It is so easy! Much easier than using a brush because firstly the control is more effective and closer and, secondly, the pressure is more sensitive and accurate.

Moreover, the fingers smooth the paint so that it is easier to paint a detail in light colour over an area which has been treated with the fingers. I have done this when painting the edges of the rose-petals: first, using a no. 4 flat brush, I speckled the dark colours, the shaded areas of the rose and carmine parts, keeping the model in view. Then I worked over the same areas with the tip of my third and little fingers, blending, shading and smoothing. Finally, I had only to paint with a sable brush loaded with undiluted white, red and carmine paint straight from the tube, in order to obtain whatever results I wanted.

---

24. — Can you go on by yourself now?

One last piece of advice:

DON'T GO ON TOO LONG.

There is nothing more difficult than to stop in time, to cease painting before the work becomes fussy, precious and expressionless. An unpolished sketchy finish is a thousand times better.

The famous artist, Gauguin, said in this connection: «Do not put too much finish on your work. A good impression only lasts when the initial freshness survives a lengthy search for tiny details».

25. — Now sign it. Not too big and in a quiet colour. Then, after a few days, you can varnish the painting, if you want.

26. — VARNISHING A PICTURE

The reasons for varnishing a picture are as follows:

1. To protect the paint from dirt and dust (since an oil-varnish can safely be washed) although the best protection is provided by glass. 2. To increase the brilliance and strength of the colours which have remained matt owing either to their composition or to being diluted with too much white spirit. 3. As a corollary to 2), to give equal strength and brilliance to all the colours in the picture.

Many modern artists do not use varnish since they prefer a matt finish which is obtained by leaving out some or all the linseed oil as a solvent and also by using an absorbent support such as cardboard and wood with matt priming.

The main drawback of varnish is, in fact, its primary quality: its shine. Under certain conditions, this can prevent a proper view of the picture.

Varnish for painting is sold in bottles ready for use. Before applying it, the picture must be absolutely dry. This takes a month or so. The varnish is applied by a broad flat brush which should be sable, but hog brushes can be used.

And so...

But sit down, you must be tired. So am I, I'll admit. Painting is tiring. In his play «Orpheus Descending», Tennessee Williams, the famous American playwright, gave one of his characters a speech about how tiring painting can be.

«I been painting all day, finished a picture in a
ten-hour stretch, just stopped a few minutes fo'
coffee and went back to it again while I had a
clear vision... I'm so exhausted I could drop in my
tracks. There's nothing more exhausting on earth,
than that kind of work, it's not so much that it tires
your body out, but it leaves you drained inside.
Y'know what I mean? Like you was burned out by
something Still! You feel you've accomplished
something when you're through with it, sometimes you
feel — elevated.»